Suicide

Psychological Disorders

Psychological
Disorders

Suicide

Ron Salomon, M.D.

Series Editor
Christine Collins, Ph.D.
Research Assistant Professor of Psychology
Vanderbilt University

Foreword by
Pat Levitt, Ph.D.
Director, Vanderbilt Kennedy Center
for Research on Human Development

CHELSEA HOUSE
PUBLISHERS
An imprint of Infobase Publishing

Psychological Disorders: Suicide

Chelsea House
An imprint of Infobase Publishing
132 West 31st Street
New York NY 10001

Library of Congress Cataloging-in-Publication Data
Suicide / Ron Salomon ; consulting editor, Christine Collins ; foreword by Pat Levitt.
    p. ; cm. — (Psychological disorders)
  Includes bibliographical references and index.
  ISBN-13: 978-0-7910-9007-7 (alk. paper)
  ISBN-10: 0-7910-9007-8 (alk. paper)
  1. Suicidal behavior. I. Salomon, Ron. II. Collins, Christine E. (Christine Elaine)
III. Title. IV. Series: Psychological disorders (Chelsea House Publishers)
  [DNLM: 1. Suicide. 2. Adolescent. WM 165 S9472 2007]
  RC569.S9312 2007
  616.85'8445—dc22   2007010992

You can find Chelsea House on the World Wide Web at http://www.chelseahouse.com

Text design by Keith Trego
Cover design by Keith Trego and Ben Peterson

Printed in the United States of America

Bang EJB 10 9 8 7 6 5 4 3 2 1

This book is printed on acid-free paper.

All links and Web addresses were checked and verified to be correct at the time of publication. Because of the dynamic nature of the Web, some addresses and links may have changed since publication and may no longer be valid.

Table of Contents

Foreword

Pat Levitt, Ph.D.
Vanderbilt Kennedy
Center for Research
on Human Development

Think of the most complicated aspect of our universe, and then multiply that by infinity! Even the most enthusiastic of mathematicians and physicists acknowledge that the brain is by far the most challenging entity to understand. By design, the human brain is made up of billions of cells called neurons, which use chemical neurotransmitters to communicate with each other through connections called synapses. Each brain cell has about 2,000 synapses. Connections between neurons are not formed in a random fashion, but rather are organized into a type of architecture that is far more complex than any of today's supercomputers. And, not only is the brain's connective architecture more complex than any computer; its connections are capable of *changing* to improve the way a circuit functions. For example, the way we learn new information involves changes in circuits that actually improve performance. Yet some change can also result in a disruption of connections, like changes that occur in disorders such as drug addiction, depression, schizophrenia, and epilepsy, or even changes that can increase a person's risk of suicide.

Genes and the environment are powerful forces in building the brain during development and ensuring normal brain functioning, but they can also be the root causes of psychological and neurological disorders when things go awry. The way in which brain architecture is built before birth and in childhood will determine how well the brain functions when we are adults, and even how susceptible we are to such diseases as depression, anxiety, or attention disorders, which can severely disturb brain function. In a sense, then, understanding how the brain is built can lead us to a clearer picture of the ways in which our brain works, how we can improve its functioning, and what we can do to repair it when diseases strike.

Brain architecture reflects the highly specialized jobs that are performed by human beings, such as seeing, hearing, feeling, smelling, and moving. Different brain areas are specialized to control specific functions. Each specialized area must communicate well with other areas for the brain to accomplish even more complex tasks, like controlling body physiology—our patterns of sleep, for example, or even our eating habits, both of which can become disrupted if brain development or function is disturbed in some way. The brain controls our feelings, fears, and emotions; our ability to learn and store new information; and how well we recall old information. The brain does all this, and more, by building, during development, the circuits that control these functions, much like a hard-wired computer. Even small abnormalities that occur during early brain development through gene mutations, viral infection, or fetal exposure to alcohol can increase the risk of developing a wide range of psychological disorders later in life.

Those who study the relationship between brain architecture and function, and the diseases that affect this bond, are neuroscientists. Those who study and treat the disorders that are caused by changes in brain architecture and chemistry are psychiatrists and psychologists. Over the last 50 years, we have learned quite a lot about how brain architecture and chemistry work and how genetics contribute to brain structure and function. Genes are very important in controlling the initial phases of building the brain. In fact, almost every gene in the human genome is needed to build the brain. This process of brain development actually starts prior to birth, with almost all the neurons we will ever have in our brain produced by mid-gestation. The assembly of the architecture, in the form of intricate circuits, begins by this time, and by birth, we have the basic organization laid out. But the work is not yet complete, because billions of connections form over a remarkably long period of time, extending through puberty. The brain of a child is being built and modified on a daily basis, even during sleep.

While there are thousands of chemical building blocks, such as proteins, lipids, and carbohydrates, that are used, much like bricks and mortar, to put the architecture together, the highly detailed connectivity that emerges during childhood depends greatly upon experiences and our environment. In building a house, we use specific blueprints to assemble the basic structures, like a foundation, walls, floors, and ceilings. The brain is assembled similarly. Plumbing and electricity, like the basic circuitry of the brain, are put in place early in the building process. But for all of this early work, there is another very important phase of development, which is termed experience-dependent development. During the first three years of life, our brains actually form far more connections than we will ever need, almost 40 percent more! Why would this occur? Well, in fact, the early circuits form in this way so that we can use experience to mold our brain architecture to best suit the functions that we are likely to need for the rest of our lives

Experience is not just important for the circuits that control our senses. A young child who experiences toxic stress, like physical abuse, will have his or her brain architecture changed in regions that will result in poorer control of emotions and feelings as an adult. Experience is powerful. When we repeatedly practice on the piano or shoot a basketball hundreds of times daily, we are using experience to model our brain connections to function at their finest. Some will achieve better results than others, perhaps because the initial phases of circuit-building provided a better base, just like the architecture of houses may differ in terms of their functionality. We are working to understand the brain structure and function that result from the powerful combination of genes building the initial architecture and a child's experience adding the all-important detailed touches. We also know that, like an old home, the architecture can break down. The aging process can be particularly hard on the ability of brain circuits to function at their best because positive change comes less readily as we get older. Synapses may be lost and brain chemistry can change over time. The difficulties in understanding how architecture gets built are paralleled by the complexities of what happens to that architecture as we grow older. Dementia associated with brain deterioration as a complication of Alzheimer's disease and memory loss associated with aging or alcoholism are active avenues of research in the neuroscience community.

There is truth, both for development and in aging, in the old adage "use it or lose it." Neuroscientists are pursuing the idea that brain architecture and chemistry can be modified well beyond childhood. If we understand the mechanisms that make it easy for a young, healthy brain to learn or repair itself following an accident, perhaps we can use those same tools to optimize the functioning of aging brains. We already know many ways in which we can improve the functioning of the aging or injured brain. For example, for an individual who has suffered a stroke that has caused structural damage to brain architecture, physical exercise can be quite powerful in helping to reorganize circuits so that they function better, even in an elderly individual. And you know that when you exercise and sleep regularly, you just feel better. Your brain chemistry and architecture are functioning at their best. Another example of ways we can improve nervous system function are the drugs that are used to treat mental illnesses. These drugs are designed to change brain chemistry so that the neurotransmitters used for communication between brain cells can function more normally. These same types of drugs, however, when taken in excess or abused, can actually damage brain chemistry and change brain architecture so that it functions more poorly.

As you read the Psychological Disorders series, the images of altered brain organization and chemistry will come to mind in thinking about complex diseases such as schizophrenia or drug addiction. There is nothing more fascinating and important to understand for the well-being of humans. But also keep in mind that as neuroscientists, we are on a mission to comprehend human nature, the way we perceive the world, how we recognize color, why we smile when thinking about the Thanksgiving turkey, the emotion of experiencing our first kiss, or how we can remember the winner of the 1953 World Series. If you are interested in people, and the world in which we live, you are a neuroscientist, too.

Pat Levitt, Ph.D.
Director, Vanderbilt Kennedy Center
for Research on Human Development
Vanderbilt University
Nashville, Tennessee

Reasons for Suicide

An ocean tide changes, pulling water from a bay. It is powered by invisible, natural forces that work steadily and silently, creating a totally new landscape in a matter of moments. We can't see the moon's gravity, but we see its effects on the tide. Similarly, changes in brain chemistry and thought patterns that lead to self-destructive behavior can appear to come from nowhere and dramatically change our worldviews. As we ponder our life circumstances or grieve the loss of loved ones, we can convince ourselves that things will never get any better or that life is not worth living. If we repeat these thoughts to ourselves often enough, we can come to believe they are true. But, later, looking back on those moments, such thoughts seem strange and alien. It is hard to understand where they came from and it is very necessary to understand how to keep the thoughts from coming back.

Suicide is the third leading cause of death in young people between 13 and 20 and is the 11th leading cause of death for people of all ages. Here are a few stories from suicide survivors that may help us understand the experiences of those who first contemplate, then threaten, or attempt suicide.

ABE

Those who knew Abe, including many close friends, were taken by surprise when Abe was hospitalized after shooting himself, missing vital organs by just an eighth of an inch. "My hand moved at the last second. I guess I had second thoughts just in time," Abe said. The injury healed easily, and he talked about it as if it had happened in a movie and wasn't real. "I remember thinking that I wouldn't want to face life without her [Abe's ex-girlfriend], having my friends hear that she dumped me, having to go by her place every day and think of her." When he tried to commit suicide, he had just finished talking with his ex-girlfriend for the last time. It was a spur-of-the-moment decision. "I'd had two beers. The gun was there and I just automatically picked it up, without thinking much. I thought it was the only thing I could do."

An impulsive thought, a gun, and a couple of beers make a very volatile mixture. In that brief moment life seemed unimportant to Abe, and anger, pain, sadness, and embarrassment took control of his thoughts. He forgot the positive aspects of his life, which included his brother, many friends, and his growing talents as an actor. The romantic breakup compounded his suffering from his parents' divorce five years earlier. Looking back, there were many **risk factors**, but Abe had always said he would be "okay." For Abe, the signs of danger (called risk factors) included his impulsiveness, but also that no one had ever gotten him to talk about things.

BILLIE-JO
Billie-Jo described feelings that "just built up" and overwhelmed her to a point where she said, "I just couldn't stand it anymore." She had tried to "go to sleep and not wake up" by taking more of her anxiety medication than usual. She had no idea where the feelings came from, but she felt unable to change anything. It was as if everything was stuck. She even remembered thinking that it might never rain again. Even though the thought made no sense, she remembered feeling quite convinced that a drought was coming that would last forever.

Billie-Jo was suffering from severe anxiety. **Anxiety** is an illness that can be measured with imaging scans and other scientific tools. It isn't just in the imagination. It can become so powerful that people like Billie-Jo seek to escape by committing suicide. This is terribly unfortunate because there are many effective treatments that can relieve the symptoms of anxiety. Panic disorder, one specific form of anxiety, is especially associated with suicidal behavior. Like Billie-Jo's thoughts about drought, panic and other anxiety symptoms are illogical. Even though these thoughts don't make sense, they are persistent, powerful, and tremendously damaging to a person's health, social life, and performance in school or at work. Stress, including stress from anxiety, is considered a risk factor for heart disease, and has been associated with poor healing from infections, surgeries, and cancer. The social lives of persons with untreated anxiety disorders are often solitary and unsatisfying. While some persons with untreated anxiety can overcome them enough to perform well academically, they often have difficulty with tasks that involve teamwork.

These disorders are common: about 40 million (about one in eight) adults are affected,[1] and the Anxiety Disorders Association of America (ADAA) Web site gets 5 million hits per month. Among teens, anxiety usually takes the form of generalized anxiety disorder and social anxiety disorder. Adolescents sometimes also have panic disorder, and obsessive-compulsive disorder may begin at any age. *All of these disorders are highly responsive to treatment.* Treatment should be sought long before suicide becomes even a distant thought.

CARLA

There are such "terrible swings in my moods," Carla said. "I had them under control and stopped the medicine about six months ago because I was *sure* I was all better and that they wouldn't come back." She felt fine until one month prior to her suicide attempt when she started to feel like no one could ever love her. She said the feeling "must be wrong" because she was as sure as anyone could be of her religious faith and her strong connection to her family. But the thoughts and feelings came anyway. Carla attempted suicide because she "could see the old pattern coming back" and didn't want to experience these feelings again. At its worst, the depression had immobilized her. She tried suicide this time before the depression got too bad, anxiously trying to avoid reexperiencing it at its worst.

Mood illnesses can be treated successfully, bringing most people fully back to "normal," whatever that might be to them. Yet, like teens, about 20 to 30 percent of adults who have depression will not get completely better. Symptoms sometimes cycle on and off over months or years. Early in a mood illness there is a tendency for people to feel overly hopeful and stop taking their medications. Optimism is good (and a very human trait), but stopping medications as Carla did is known to be risky.

Carla had lost perspective in two ways, something she realized later. First, after recovering from two previous episodes of serious depression, she had forgotten the success of her treatment, which demonstrates an important point about memory and **mood states**. What we remember depends on a number of factors, including mood. Depressed people can't remember the good times. And when people are feeling good, they may stop their treatment, partly because the memories of bad times fade. When she had the depression again and the illness was doing her thinking for her, Carla forgot the good results of her treatment for depression.

Carla's other loss of perspective had to do with her sense of being loved. She realized that it made no sense to feel that way,

Depression

The formal name for depression is major depressive disorder, and it has several subtypes. All of them have similar symptoms, including periods of severe sad, low moods that can come and go for weeks at a time. Sometimes an episode starts without a clear provocation or trigger. Episodes of depression will usually go away slowly on their own in about six months, but resolve more quickly with treatment. Depression comes back more easily the more times it has occurred. Between episodes of depression, normal moods can return and there may be no sign of the prior sadness. Sometimes,

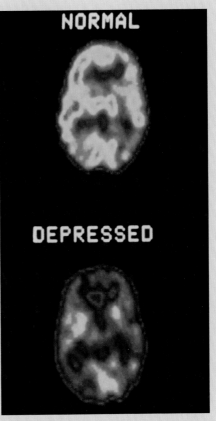

Figure 1.1 Brain PET scans indicating the difference in levels and locations of brain activity in healthy and depressed individuals. © *Science VU/DOE/Visuals Unlimited*

however, people with depression also have periods of dysthymia, feeling halfway down, in between the full-blown depressions. People with dysthymia may remind you of the loveable donkey Eeyore in the Winnie the Pooh books, who always seems to be feeling low but is not quite depressed.

since she had a very loving and caring family, and she knew that she was lucky. Her parents were healthy, and she had a good relationship with her older sister. It is common for people to find their negative thoughts illogical (which they are), or sometimes to judge themselves as selfish (which they are not).

Depression is not something people create by themselves. It is not deserved as punishment, and it is not something that anyone wants to experience. But depression does create negative ideas, including the thought that one is being selfish. It's all part of depression itself, and when a person gets better, thinking gets more positive, including the sense of being loved.

Carla missed the warning signs that her depressive symptoms were recurring, but will learn to watch for them in the future. Early interventions and treatments are important for first episodes, and also if or when the symptoms come back.

DAVID

David said that it had become clear; there was almost a single sudden moment when he was sure. He was no longer in doubt of his sexual orientation. But he was just as sure that no one and especially not his parents could even begin to suspect that he was gay. Would there be anyone besides his friend Erica who could know that he was having suicidal thoughts? What a crazy world it was becoming—he had always prided himself on being open and friendly, never needing to hide anything.

Having the insulin shots for diabetes every day had already caused plenty of strife in the family. His mom was a nervous wreck, and he was sure it was all because of his disease. He thought, *She probably blames herself, for God's sake.* But it wasn't anyone's fault. Diabetes just happens. *Being gay,* he thought, *was something you could wish on yourself,* even though he didn't really believe it. His dad was nice to him but hadn't made much effort to be involved in the finger sticks and insulin shots. Work, golf, and sometimes hunting kept his father's calendar full. Andy, his older brother, was the star athlete in track, popular with everyone, and was always taken along on hunting trips while David stayed home with the diabetes and his mom. If they all found out, it would tear the household apart forever and they'd always hate and reject him. *They would get over his death much more easily,* he thought, *than get used to living with his being gay.*

Teens usually reveal suicidal thoughts to peers, and not to parents, teachers, counselors, or religious leaders. Erica kept his secret, and he had kept his promise to her that he wouldn't leave her without saying goodbye. She couldn't let him go, and convinced him to call a therapist who had visited her church to talk about depression in teens. David knew that having such a limited network of friends was risky, but having her listen and still like him gave him a little hope. Talking with Erica about suicide saved his life.

David had a number of issues to work through for which therapy was likely to be very helpful. The therapist encouraged him to explore different ways of defining his needs, expressing himself constructively, and setting appropriate goals for the coming high school and college years. These years require many adjustments as the "inner child" grows into adulthood, keeping an inner character and yet developing a more refined, self-defined presentation to the outside world. The additional stresses due to David's chronic illness and sexual orientation made this transition more complex but certainly achievable. He'll look back someday on this time as a chapter of growth during which his adult persona was framed. Therapy helped as he worked through this period.

MENTAL DISORDERS AND INTERNAL RISK FACTORS

Mental health professionals attach very specific meanings to words that describe emotion, so that people can become clearer about what is meant by terms like *anxiety* or *depression*, which will be discussed in depth later in the book. The term **mental disorders** refers to all of the illnesses of the brain that occur without the obvious damage of neurological disorders such as stroke, brain cancer, or brain damage from an accident. However, individual mental disorders are difficult to define because words for emotions are often used in many ways. For example, the term *nervous breakdown* can be used to describe a fit of hysterical laughter and giddy happiness that lasts a few hours after some particularly good news, or it can mean a severe psychotic condition that requires long-term hospitalization. Higher risks of suicide are associated with certain mental disorders, including depression, bipolar disorder, drug use disorders, and conduct disorder. It is also important to know that even if diagnostic names for a person's symptoms are not always perfectly clear, they are often useful for helping medical professionals choose the best treatment. Even if a name for the mental disorder isn't exactly clear, it is possible to find successful treatments for the symptoms that arise.

About 70 to 80 percent of suicides have occurred in individuals who had diagnoses of either depression or alcohol dependence, or both. A severe mental illness, **schizophrenia**, accounts for 5 percent of all suicides, which might sound small, but this is a very high rate considering the small number of people who have that illness. Another 15 percent of individuals who die of suicide had other psychiatric illnesses, including anxiety disorders.

SUICIDE RISK—THE EXTERNAL FACTORS

Besides depression and other mental illnesses, several outside factors also affect the risk of suicide. Events such as personal illness, illnesses or deaths in the family, abuse during childhood, and divorce are stressful for everyone who undergoes them. The

Diagnoses as Guides to Risk Factors for Suicide

Surveys conducted in the Smoky Mountains region of the south-eastern United States have shown the relationship between suicide in youth and the presence of specific psychiatric illnesses, or diagnoses (diagnoses are standardized tools used to specifically describe illnesses to aid doctors in choosing treatments). These data were collected from interviews of 1,420 students and their parents over a period of about eight years, and analyzed by Drs. Debra Foley, David Goldston, Jane Costello, and Adrian Angold.[2] They found that when youths met the criteria for specific diagnoses, especially more than one diagnosis, risk factors for suicidal thoughts and behaviors increased greatly. These results warn that even if symptoms of certain illnesses appear to be mild, risks can be very high.

1. Current depression plus anxiety, specifically generalized anxiety disorder, gives an increase in risk by more than a factor of four hundred and fifty. (Odds ratio = 468)

2. Depression plus a disruptive disorder increases risk more than two-hundred-fold (Odds ratio = 223). *Disruptive disorder* is a term used for oppositional, defiant, and other behaviors that appear continuously, with or without mood changes.

3. Substance use disorders increase risk when they occur in addition to other disorders such as depression or one of the bipolar disorders.

4. More severe symptoms generally increase the risk of suicide, but not necessarily more than when depression and generalized anxiety disorder were present together. This combination brought high risk regardless of perceptions of the symptom severity.

Figure 1.2 A scene from *Leave It to Beaver*, a show that stressed emotional intimacy and bonding between family members. © *ABC/Photofest*

way people manage stress has changed dramatically over the past five decades. The idealized family model has moved from *Leave It to Beaver* and *The Waltons*, where families seemed to be together almost all the time, to *One Tree Hill* and *The Real World*, where most emotional exchanges occur among peers. These cultural changes appear to be associated with increases in substance use and a greater frequency of depressive symptoms, including suicidal behaviors especially among young people. Many researchers believe that the shift away from family cohesiveness may account for the slow progress in preventing suicide even though considerable effort has been given to recognition of and treatment for people at risk.

People give many sorts of reasons for their suicide attempts, but a common thread is that people contemplate suicide when they feel hopeless. Only later, when the whole picture is examined, do they admit that the hopelessness that triggered the suicide attempt is not justified and doesn't make sense. Stress in the family, legal problems, school or work problems, and social pressures can trigger a switch in mood, but most people are able to bounce back in an hour, or a day or two at most. With suicidal depression, however, the low moods persist for too long, and the rebound is not easy.

SUICIDE RISK—THE SUBSTANCE ABUSE FACTOR

Substances of abuse are initially external factors, but once started, they literally and figuratively become internal factors. Cigarette smoking, independent of other substance use, increases the liability for suicidal behavior. Alcohol is involved in about 50 percent of all suicide attempts. It may seem to diminish the stress initially, but it is a depressant, making problems worse with repeated use. Alcohol's adverse effects on the brain go beyond mood control problems. One study by Jerome Yesavage

Figure 1.3 An alcoholic man standing in an alley with a beer in his hand. Alcohol abuse has a strong correlation with suicide attempts. © *Jim Varney/ Photo Researchers, Inc.*

and Van Leirer in 1986 asked a group of test pilots—all in their mid-20s, all in top physical and mental condition, and all accustomed to drinking regularly—to *abstain* from drinking for two days. After the two days, the researchers had the pilots do some tests of coordination and thinking skills using a flight simulator, and then gave them several shots of any liquor they wanted, enough to just reach the legal limit of blood alcohol. The tests were repeated after 14 hours, and even then the pilots' skills had not returned to baseline.[3] The pilots' hangovers appeared to last for almost a day, not just an hour or two, and long after the pilots were no longer legally intoxicated. More recent studies also show that chemical signals in the brain are disrupted for many days even after a short binge. The chemical disruption lasts longer than the binge that caused them.

Why are moods and memories affected by alcohol? The parts of the brain involved in memory and mood (the hippocampal formation and the frontal cortex) are about the size of your fist, and the parts that control movement and coordination (the motor cortex) are about the size of your index finger. The memory and mood parts are not only larger but also much more complex, and they need to work together in a much more complicated way. If the motor cortex can't work properly for almost a day after a small amount of alcohol, there's not much chance that the emotional areas are going to work well.

Drug use is another suicide risk factor. The suicides of many famous people are often accompanied by stories of drug and alcohol abuse or prescription drug misuse. There is often connection between a glamorous lifestyle and substance use, but if examined carefully, these lives are also full of heartbreak and personal tragedy. Drug addictions are difficult to heal, even with help. The notes that suicidal celebrities leave behind, talking about their loneliness, isolation, and lost ability to enjoy life, always baffle their fans. It just doesn't make sense to us. How could they be missing out when they have so much?

SUICIDE AND TREATMENT

Research studies and the experiences of patients who have survived a suicide attempt show improvements with treatment.

Abe can be expected to benefit from **talk therapy**, in which he would meet with a trained therapist to understand why his relationship with his ex-girlfriend led him to experience such self-destructive feelings, as well as to recognize and minimize the factors that increase his risk. A mild medication might be considered under the supervision of a specialist.

Billie-Jo had been through several cycles of a recurring illness. For her, a longer time in treatment could be recommended, involving intermittent talk therapy added to long-term, anti-anxiety medication. Treatment would be expected to prevent the sudden and severe changes in her mood that cause her to panic or feel extremely anxious. In therapy, she would also learn how to

Warning Signs for Suicidal Risk in Adolescents

There are many myths about suicide, oftentimes falsely reassuring. A list of suicide warning signs was published by Dr. Keith King in the *Journal of School Health* almost a decade ago.[4] It is still pertinent today, even though rates are beginning to fall from a peak in the 1990s.

1. Depressed mood
2. Substance abuse
3. Loss of interest in pleasurable activities
4. Decreased activity levels
5. Decreased attention
6. Distractibility
7. Isolation
8. Withdrawal from others
9. Sleep changes
10. Appetite changes
11. Morbid ideation (thinking about hurting oneself or dying)
12. Verbal cues, such as saying "I wish I were dead"
13. Written cues like notes or poems
14. Giving possessions away

prevent anxiety and minimize her reactions to changes and their effects on her daily life.

Carla's wish to feel well without medication might not be easily achieved, because people with her symptoms are able to better control their lives by staying in treatment and continuing their medications. The medications for her would probably have few difficult side effects, mostly the daily annoyance of needing to remember to take them.

David will have a great deal to discuss in therapy and will learn that his problems may be difficult but are not at all insurmountable, and that his family would much rather learn to adjust than to lose him. He will likely find that his thoughtful nature will be highly valued among friends throughout his life.

Again, the given reasons for suicide attempts often don't make sense later to the person who had the thoughts in the first place. Thoughts can become confused with mental illness, or the external environment can become confusing. Even though mental illness is present in almost everyone who attempts or completes a suicide, only a minority of people with mental illness commit suicide. The worries and confusions that trigger an attempt can be difficult to understand even after only a week has passed. In retrospect, Abe's longtime friends had never liked his ex-girlfriend because Abe seemed too involved with her and didn't seem like himself when he was with her, so why did the breakup become so devastating to him? For Billie-Jo, anxiety and depression got better with treatment and she started really wanting to live, not disappear. Carla learned that it made sense to stay on her medication even when she felt well. David understood that his family loved him for who he was, not for who he thought they wanted him to be. For all of these people, there will be good moments that will come along and make even their struggles worthwhile, and the escape from momentary woes through suicide will become completely unnecessary.

Hidden historical risk factors—the things we don't often think about—can also contribute to a person's chances of becoming suicidal. A history of physical or sexual abuse during childhood has been associated with greater risk.[5] A history of someone in the family who had attempted suicide, even very long ago, remains a strong factor. It should not be surprising that certain historical factors, such as a person's prior attempts, remain a risk factor even decades later. Having a serious head injury or neurological disease also raise risks. Other factors, especially those that affect teens, will be discussed in other chapters. The important thing to remember is that there is help.

Impulses, Emotions, and Unexpected Behaviors

Abe hadn't woken up on the day of his suicide attempt with the intention to kill himself. His actions that evening were entirely impulsive. There was no note, no real premeditation, and no obvious depression or anxiety. Just some beer, a gun, and a bad breakup. Abe had grown up around guns and always thought he knew how to respect them. Several weeks after trying to kill himself with the gun, Abe was still shocked that he had so suddenly lost touch with himself, forgotten everything he had learned about gun safety, and become completely unaware of everyone he loved.

In Abe's situation, it seems as if no one could have predicted that moment of sudden violence. But if we take a closer look, there may be some clues. In some ways, Abe's impulse may not have been such a surprise after all.

CHEMICAL IMBALANCES AND SUICIDE

Impulsive behavior can take many forms in a reaction to a stressful event. Some people who attempt suicide show difficulty controlling their impulses, but not all suicides are impulsive and not all impulses are suicidal. Obviously, other impulsive behaviors can be very damaging, too, such as trichotillomania (people who habitually pull out their hair), sexual offenses (abuse of children or rape), impulse buying, gambling, or arson (setting fires). Yet it may be that each of these behaviors are associated with similarly abnormal chemical functions in the brain. The treatments for impulse control problems, both talking therapies and medication, have been shown to change chemical systems in the brain. Medications are often needed for severe problems to assist with restoring normal self-control of brain activity patterns. The combination of medication and talk therapies is usually the best approach.

Clues about chemical imbalances are gradually leading to **genes** that are coded in our DNA (deoxyribonucleic acid) and might influence behavior quite powerfully. Several different chemical pathways seem to be involved. **Serotonin** is one of the major **neurotransmitter** substances. Neurotransmitters are chemicals that brain cells use to communicate with one another, and they can be measured in cerebrospinal fluid, which surrounds the brain and spinal cord. Considerable research shows that one major chemical abnormality in the brain associated with impulsive behavior is a low **turnover** of serotonin. Turnover is shown by the level of the serotonin **metabolite** (breakdown product), which is usually measured by taking small samples of the cerebrospinal fluid from the lower spine area. This is the safest place for removing samples of the fluid. Serotonin is present throughout the body but is especially abundant in the brain, blood-vessel walls, and intestines. Most of the medicines that seem to help with impulsivity, and certain other psychological symptoms, act by adjusting the activity of serotonin in the brain. A great deal of study focuses on serotonin-regulating systems to find better ways to help them work normally.

Many studies of the brain chemistry of suicide victims have been conducted over the last half century and found low levels of a serotonin metabolite called 5-hydroxyindoleacetic acid (5-HIAA). This work suggests that it is very likely serotonin neurotransmitter systems are involved in suicide, but that a large number of genes play a role and finding the crucial ones is a

Figure 2.1 Graphic of the neurotransmitter serotonin. Low levels of serotonin have been found in suicide victims. © *Alfred Pasieka/Photo Researchers, Inc.*

puzzle. Monozygotic (identical) and dizygotic (fraternal) twin studies confirmed that genes play a strong role. Several estimates suggest that genes and environmental factors are about equally responsible for suicidal behavior risks. Some genes probably relate to mental illnesses such as depression, and other genes may add aggressive or impulsive traits.

Although there are numerous possibilities among the many genes involved in brain chemistry, when one of these genes was studied by two different methods, a great deal was learned. In recent work, two groups of researchers using two different study designs were able to show that a particular gene is regulated differently in depressed people. The regulatory part of this gene is called *SLC6A4*. It is located on the long arm of chromosome 17 (the exact address, for genetics mavens, is *17q11.2*) and it controls activation of the part of the gene that codes for synthesis of the transporter. This transporter is found in serotonin **synapses,** the junctions between certain nerve cells where nerve impulses are transmitted. The transporter sweeps serotonin back into the cell that sent it out in the first place so that it can be reused, controlling turnover.

A group working in England, Wisconsin, and New Zealand studied a large number of people over several years to see if a relationship exists between the codes in the regulatory part of the gene and responses to life stressors. Dr. Avshalom Caspi and his colleagues found that life stress combined with a relatively common variation in this regulatory gene predicted more frequent depressive symptoms, depression, and suicidal tendencies.[6]

Just shortly before that study was published, a separate research project at the National Institute of Mental Health in the United States showed a similar relationship between activity of that same gene, symptoms of depression, and brain scan results. Drs. Ahmad Hariri and Danny Weinberger and their colleagues used a method called **functional magnetic resonance imaging**, which shows changes in the energy and activity (reflecting oxygen use) of specific parts of the brain. In these studies, the researchers showed associations between reduced serotonin transporter expression and function and increased fear and anxiety-related behaviors.[7] They also found greater neuronal activity in the **amygdala**, a small almond-sized brain region just below and behind the eyes that controls behaviors such as mood, anxiety, and anger. To measure this, Hariri and Weinberger compared individuals who carry different forms of this gene. Depending on the form of the gene, the researchers saw increases or decreases in activity in the amygdala when the subjects saw pictures of people with frightened expressions.

The findings of both these studies, that environment and genes together strongly influence our behavior, has already been supported in more than one hundred studies all over the world within the last few years. Other studies have found several other genes that, along with stress in the environment, have powerful effects on our behaviors (see Table 2.1).

Such studies are showing that stressful events interact with many genes from several families of transmitter systems. Table 2.1 discusses a selection of many findings related only to the serotonin family, and by the time this book is printed, it will certainly be out of date. If certain genes that influence suicide and high levels of stress are present, the risks of suicide appear to become higher. Several other variant genes and transmitter systems have been found in people with depression. Subtypes of depression might be determined by different sets of variant genes, but the same variant genes might also be found in different mental illnesses. A large number of factors appear to come into play, including multiple gene variants, the type of stress that occurs, and the timing of the gene-stress interaction. Genes are turned on and off throughout our lives, so they may leave people vulnerable to stress at specific times. If someone gets through that period without a great deal of stress, the undesirable effects of that gene might never be expressed.

We know nothing about Abe's genes, and even if we did, we would not know how to fix the gene patterns safely. Maybe in the future we'll be able to use that information to help people with a genetic predisposition to an illness so that stress in the environment doesn't cause dysfunctional symptoms to emerge. Until then, there is other information that we can use to help Abe.

Table 2.1 Examples of Serotonin-Related Candidate Genes Investigated in Suicidal Behavior[8]

GENE	FUNCTION	VARIANT	STUDY FINDINGS
Tryptophan hydroxylase (TPH1, TPH2)	Enzyme that makes serotonin	Changes in enzyme structure and function	Association with suicidal behavior
Monoamine oxidase A (MAOA)	Enzyme that breaks down extra serotonin	Changes activity due to changes in regulator gene	Existence of impulsive-aggressive, violent traits
Serotonin transporter (5-HTTLPR, SLC6A4)	Pulls serotonin back to the sending cell for reuse	Promoter gene activity regulates construction of the transporter	Increased likelihood of violent and repeated suicide attempts
5-HT1A receptor	Gives back information to the sending cell	Increased numbers in synapses but no difference in gene sequences	Gene not associated
5-HT1B receptor	Input for receiving cell	Few studies have been done	May be associated with violence
5-HT2A receptor	Major input for the receiving cell	Increased receptor numbers in synapses; few candidate gene changes have been studied	No clear association

GUNS, BEER, AND IMPULSES

It does not seem difficult to determine that mixing guns, beer, and impulsivity might be a bad idea. Then again, they are all quite common and easily obtained. Beer is found nearly everywhere. Guns are present in about 40 percent of American households (among the highest in the developed world), and most of those weapons are not safely locked up. Impulsive decisions are a mainstay of our consumerism—they're the reason why advertising occupies so much television time. Impulsive decisions are a part of the American lifestyle and that's not likely to change anytime soon. Some impulses turn out to have good outcomes, but others cause terrible tragedies. Again, how can we help someone like Abe when all of these things are so ubiquitous?

COPING AND COMMUNICATING

Abe had shunned professional help when his parents got divorced several years before the attempt. No one strongly urged him at that time to seek help in dealing with his changing family circumstances, even though his grades slipped and he was more withdrawn and quiet in school for a couple of years. Children and adolescents don't always show the same signs and symptoms of depression as adults do. Grades can drop, they seem withdrawn, and it goes on not just for a day or two, but for weeks or months. Moods come and go, which can seem normal to most parents of teenagers. After all, teens are expected to be moody. Sleep habits change wildly during adolescence, and Abe's periods of sleeping too much seemed normal for those couple of years. It's also quite common for preteens and teens to change their groups of friends once in a while, so Abe's sudden strong attachment to his new girlfriend didn't seem terribly unusual.

Therapy after his suicide attempt was quite helpful for Abe. He came to recognize that he had been through a series of bouts with depression starting around the time of his parents' first separation. The first episode had been ignored when it began and rapidly peaked and subsided but was never quite resolved. Recently he had seemed perfectly fine to all his current friends but no one from that group, and certainly none of his girlfriend's friends, had known him in the years before his parents' separation. As he looked back, he realized that his memories of feeling happy came from times that were long before the divorce. He remembered thinking to himself that it was normal to feel low at the time of the separation. He kept quiet and never let out his anger or tears. He tried to pretend the anger wasn't even there. Both he and his parents accepted his changes as a normal result of the stress from the divorce or just being a teenager. Abe remembered having thoughts of suicide when his parents first separated, and even then he knew where the gun was kept. Had no gun been available, he had also thought of other ways to escape his torment. He had those thoughts but never believed he would act on them. That first episode had been several years ago. His suicidal thoughts had been gone for a long time.

THOUGHTS, LOGIC, AND UNPLANNED EVENTS

The isolation of Abe's anger and sadness about the divorce set a dangerous pattern for him. Whenever an inconvenient emotion came up, he would put it away and pretend it wasn't there. He stopped showing much emotion about anything, and drinking beer in social situations seemed to help keep that lid tight, so no one could see what was going on inside. Abe had fallen instantly for his new girlfriend even though they didn't have the same friends or even similar interests. She was one of the prettiest girls he had ever seen, someone he had thought was out of his league. They had bumped into each other at an ice cream place near school when no one else was around. He wasn't trying to pick her up, just asked where all her friends were. When she answered that he could be her friend, he thought all his prayers had been answered.

They were both giddy about their romance for two or three weeks. As time went on, however, she and her friends made seemingly harmless fun of him and his less affluent background. Even so, they seemed to respect him because he could handle a few beers, tolerated their giggling about him, and was cool and good-looking. On the other hand, when Abe and his girlfriend were with his friends, he felt completely himself, just like in the days before he'd met her.

It got to a point where, at least for the moments when they were close, his girlfriend meant more to Abe than his family and friends did. His fleeting suicidal thoughts from years past seemed more distant when he was with her. She said that she loved him. He felt excitement and a strong desire to be alive and with her. It was a very intense feeling and it gave him a sense of personal safety again. He hadn't really felt that way since his parents' divorce. That all collapsed suddenly when they broke up.

For some observers, Abe had no prior plan or active suicidal thoughts, so his sudden act might seem to lack the markings of a real suicide attempt. Sometimes the same suicide attempt event could be called normal behavior by one observer, accidental by another, and self-destructive by a third person. After the fact, with no witnesses to an event, it can be difficult to decide whether an act was actually suicide or not.

PREVENTING IMPULSIVE ACTIONS

There are many ways that Abe could have sought help or talked with someone about the way he was feeling. Many local groups work to understand and prevent suicide, and the Web sites of the American Foundation for Suicide Prevention (AFSB) and other organizations have many resources to help (see Further Resources at the end of this book). Besides research on changes in brain chemistry in suicidal people, which is a major effort in many countries, there are many community resources and programs especially geared toward suicide prevention. Religious leaders are dedicated to helping anyone who is distressed. Workers in local medical doctors' offices and school guidance offices are on the lookout for suicidal behavior, but it's very hard to catch, in part because the people who need help often withdraw from social life. Detecting the truly high-risk situations and then responding effectively continue to be major goals of research and clinical outreach programs.

RISKS ACROSS THE LIFE CYCLE

Researchers learned long ago that certain age groups have a higher risk of suicide compared to other age groups. For young people ages 15 to 25, the annual suicide rate is about 10 in 10,000, and for people over 65 the rate is about 16 per 10,000. Rates for adults between these ages are lower. Programs and Web sites, crisis phone lines for teens, and social centers for the elderly have been established and are helping many people regain control of their lives. Lower suicide rates and improved quality of life are the main goals of these programs.

The major obstacle to suicide prevention appears to be poor communication. Everyone needs to learn how to tell someone when help is needed, and also how to hear and respond to the calls for help from others. Talking about ourselves is more difficult than talking about others, especially when it is about something that is strange and frightening, like suicidal thoughts. Victims often dismiss the seriousness of these thoughts at first, believing that things will eventually get better. For most people, their hopes are at least partially fulfilled and suicidal thoughts become a more distant idea, at least for a while. But things do not always get better soon enough, and the self-destructive ideas can come back, often getting larger and more insistent as they get repeated. The danger of suicide can become critical very suddenly, so seeking help early is the best way to manage the risk factors.

We can do something about the risk factor of poor communication. People in treatment have a better chance of avoiding suicide. Therapy teaches communication and is a positive factor that can help to balance out negatives from impulsivity, genes, alcohol, and stressful life events. Also, therapists routinely communicate about guns being available, and will encourage them to be removed, so it is possible that therapy helps with the risk factor of guns, too.

Abe couldn't see it coming that time, but with a few clues and some therapy, he and others will catch themselves before an impulse takes over. Impulses are controllable, even if stress and genes team up to make life challenging at times. Communication efforts, substance abuse education and treatment, and environmental safety measures all can help prevent suicide—they are a priority.

Anxiety and Suicide

In the therapist's office after her suicide attempt, Billie-Jo described how her feelings "built up" so that she felt overwhelmed to a point where she "just couldn't stand it anymore." After her 16th birthday she had tried to "go to sleep and not wake up" by taking more of her new medication than was prescribed. She knew that her parents would both be at work and wouldn't realize that she had missed school. She woke up woozy, nauseated, and frustrated that the overdose hadn't worked. Now she was seeing the therapist for her first visit since the overdose, and the therapist was the first to hear about what had happened. She'd been too afraid to tell her parents, and they barely seemed to notice that anything was going on.

SUICIDE IN PEOPLE WITH ANXIETY OR PANIC

Anxiety causes changes in the brain that can be measured with imaging scans and other methods. It isn't just in the imagination. Anxiety can become so powerful and frightening that people seek to escape, which is unfortunate because anxiety can improve a great deal with treatment. Panic disorder, one specific form of anxiety, is strongly associated with suicidal behavior. A person may recognize panic and other anxiety symptoms as being illogical, but they are nonetheless persistent and can be terrifying.

For Billie-Jo, suicide had been on her mind for quite a while. It never left her alone for more than a few hours at a time. Her anxiety had made it difficult or impossible to go out with friends, and many of her old friends seemed to have moved on to new activities without her. Her parents had noticed this and sent her to a therapist. About three weeks before the overdose, Billie-Jo had said to her mother, who was washing dishes after supper, "I get so lonely sometimes." Her mom had just looked at her and didn't say anything. The silence stung, although Billie-Jo realized that her mother may simply not have clearly heard the statement over the noise of the running water.

The therapist in the counseling center was pleasant, and Billie-Jo would leave each visit with a good feeling. The therapist had always said he was impressed with how much progress she was making. She was still going to school and doing more reading and crafts at home, and these activities made for good conversation in her therapy sessions. If only she could have told the therapist how much the anxiety was bothering her, and how often the suicidal thoughts came. She wanted to ask so many questions: Does everybody wish they were dead? Does everybody worry all the time, even about impossible things like the rain stopping forever? These bursts of panic were becoming more and more difficult to endure.

In the waiting room two weeks before the overdose, while Billie-Jo was coming out at the end of their discussion, the therapist told her mother that Billie-Jo might need a doctor to prescribe some medicine to help her. That comment probably was meant to be grown-up talk that Billie-Jo was not supposed to hear, but it didn't make sense to her. Why would the therapist tell her she was improving but then tell her mother she needed medication? Billie-Jo later said she had told herself she would never take pills. She thought that would mean she was crazy. She remembered feeling that this was too much.

During the drive home with her mother, neither of them knew what to say. When her medical doctor saw her, he just said that the therapist had suggested that Billie-Jo take something to ease her anxiety and depression. He gave her an antidepressant medicine, and said that she might experience side effects like nausea or headache for a few days. He also said the medicine would take a week or two to help her anxiety. He wanted to see her again in a month to make sure the medication was working.

Anxiety disorders can lead to symptoms of depression, and vice versa. The isolation from having anxiety can cause more stress, and this can bring on symptoms of depression. Depression and anxiety together create a higher risk for suicide than either of them alone.

Billie-Jo's story illustrates the increased risk of a suicide attempt during a first bout with symptoms of panic or anxiety disorders, before help is sought or becomes effective. For a while Billie-Jo had thought she might be getting depressed, but she hadn't told anyone. She and her therapist talked about her schoolwork and extracurricular activities, which seemed to be going better. Just before the attempt, while she was focusing on those activities, she had stopped thinking of herself as being depressed. The anxiety still felt very bad when she was alone or away from school, but it didn't seem to be part of depression anymore. It seemed more real. Somehow she had lost the ability to keep a perspective and look at herself. Her thoughts had become distorted. She sometimes believed the world was truly hostile and unforgiving. She even thought that her old friends, when they made attempts to smile at her in the hallways at school, were laughing at her behind her back. Normally she would have known that they all really only wanted all the best for her.

Suicidal thinking doesn't mean that someone is "only" depressed. Suicidal thoughts can be part of, or start with, an anxiety disorder. Suicides occur in the context of a number of psychiatric illnesses or diagnoses, including anxiety, depression, schizophrenia, and bipolar disorder.

PANIC

The first time Billie-Jo shopped alone in a crowded supermarket, she had nine items and was standing in an express checkout line for 10 items or less. What if the cashier counted each of the three lemons in her bag as individual items, instead of counting them all as one? She looked around. Several people, mostly men, seemed to be watching her. Had they counted her items? Would they complain? If there was a problem that held her up, her mother would become angry outside in the rain where she was waiting for Billie-Jo. She felt flushed and faint and her heart was racing. She barely managed to shuffle forward as the line advanced, feeling dizzy, now certain that everyone was watching her hyperventilate, sweat, and start to shake. Her chest was pounding and starting to hurt. Filled with overwhelming fear, she felt like she was about to die. Luckily no one said anything to her. She would have had to run out of the store, past her mother's car, through the rain to find somewhere to hide. It was all unbearable. She was sure no one would believe what she had felt, and that no one else ever had similar problems. It was too weird. She got to the car with the groceries and promised herself she would never tell anyone about what had happened. After that, she experienced a few more panic attacks like that first one in other situations, and decided to stop going out except for school.

Sometimes a panic attack like that makes people seem irritable or moody and depressed, but the panic is invisible and hard to describe, and goes away almost as quickly as it came. As a result, parents or friends might think that the problem is mood swings and might suspect bipolar disorder. Billie-Jo

Figure 3.1 Photo of a woman having a panic attack. Panic disorder is strongly linked to suicidal behavior. *© Pierre Perrin/Corbis SYGMA*

might be having both, and doctors know that it is common for people with bipolar disorder to also have panic attacks. Both can be helped very much with treatment.

GETTING TREATMENT

Suicide can occur without a diagnosable illness being present, but most researchers believe that the 10 percent of suicides in apparently healthy individuals are probably related to an illness that is hidden or not showing typical symptoms. Psychological distress is quite common, ranging from about 7 to 12 percent of the adult population, depending on the region of the country. Common sense suggests that adolescent levels of distress will follow closely the distress experienced in their community as a whole, but adolescent suicide data has not been mapped in this way. Suicide studies try to use very exact definitions that do not include completely accidental deaths. Suicide is an event that occurs by the person's own action or inaction with knowledge that it carries high risk of death. There are discussions about whether intent has to be absolutely clear, since sometimes the intent is difficult to prove, or it might fluctuate rapidly from one moment to the next. In any case, these suicidal "thought illnesses" almost all share a paradoxical symptom: a feeling that no one can help or understand. The paradox is that these feelings are not uncommon, so therapists *can* understand at least enough to be helpful. Almost 1 in 10 adolescents has had a serious depression that lasted at least two weeks and was of at least moderate, not just mild, severity. There are many other teens

Panic Disorder

Panic attacks are sudden, frightening spells of extreme anxiety, usually with sweating, trembling, severe sensations of shortness of breath, and a fear of "going crazy." Other symptoms like rapid heartbeat, discomfort in the chest, a choking feeling, nausea, or other fears can also occur. The spells can last for only a few minutes but cause such fear that people will run away from situations to find relief. A common trigger for these attacks can be crowded marketplaces, and if these situations are subsequently avoided, the term *agoraphobia* is used. Once people are reacting to these situations or are changing behavior because of fear of the attacks, a diagnosis of panic disorder is given. Panic disorder may appear and then go away for some patients for several years, but it often returns when stress becomes more difficult later in life. Treatment with cognitive-behavioral therapy (CBT), medications, or both is strongly recommended and highly successful.

with other forms of psychological distress. Billie-Jo is certainly not alone. Fortunately, even without a definite diagnosis, a person can still get help through therapy and many symptoms will improve rapidly. Many types of therapies and medications are available, and most people will get better with the first treatment that they try. However, since it is difficult to predict which type of therapy or medication might be best for a single individual, it is important to change once a treatment has been tried for an adequate time, at least one month, if there is absolutely no benefit. Alternative treatments are available and should be considered. Combining counseling with medication is usually the most beneficial approach.

Billie-Jo's suicide attempt with medication follows the more common pattern in women. Women are more likely to overdose on medication whereas men are more likely to attempt suicide by more violent means. Women are luckier in the outcomes, with a much higher survival rate, but the high reattempt rate remains a very threatening problem. Other things are known about the types of suicide attempts that different people might be more likely to try. Some may make suicide attempts that are less likely to be lethal than others. Often these same lower-risk attempts or gestures are attempted more frequently and present a serious risk. Low-risk suicidal gestures, even if not intended to be final, can turn deadly. Suicidal gestures or nonlethal attempts may be more common in people who frequently dramatize situations or often get into trouble with the law. It is important to remember that being a dramatic person doesn't mean someone will show suicidal behavior and it also doesn't mean that their suicidal gestures are harmless. If any person starts to mention doubts about living, even in passing, he or she must be taken very seriously. Dr. Gregory Brown and his colleagues studied the desire to live as a predictor of suicide attempts, and found that if that desire weakens, the risk of an attempt increases more that sixfold.[9] Almost half of teens who kill themselves express suicidal plans directly to someone shortly beforehand. These comments *must* be taken very seriously.

Billie-Jo might have been heading for that suicide attempt with or without the medicine. It could be that she had an unusual reaction to the medicine, or that she felt discouraged just because of embarrassment that the doctor gave it to her in the first place. It's also not clear whether the doctor remembered to specifically ask Billie-Jo about suicidal thoughts, or maybe she didn't tell her what to do if they came up. For Billie-Jo, though, the one-month follow-up visit was probably too far off. Many practitioners recommend follow-up at least at two weeks, or even weekly at the beginning of treatment. Better communication might have helped the therapist realize the growing danger underneath the superficial improvement in the schoolwork and activities.

Therapies may or may not be rapidly effective, but if they're not working after a long enough time (about four weeks), a change in therapy approach, **medications**, or both should be quickly considered. Specific dosing strategies sometimes are chosen depending on the kind of anxiety or depression that a person shows. In Billie-Jo's situation, it would be especially important to start the medications at very low doses because of the high anxiety levels. Also, the anxiety component of the illness makes it likely that the benefit from the medicine will be delayed longer than the two weeks it normally takes to alleviate depression—anxiety patients may respond in four to twelve weeks. This means that it's important to consider changing medicines carefully. Changes also carry a risk that something will be lost that was partially successful, and mental states can shift somewhat unpredictably, again requiring frequent monitoring.

Medications Used for Anxiety, Depression, Impulsive Behavior, or Bipolar Disorder

Tranquilizers—chemicals that help bring a calm feeling for short periods of time.

- GABA-boosting drugs: alcohol and benzodiazepines such as diazepam, from which addiction may result.

- Dopamine-blocking drugs: phenothiazines such as chlorpromazine and fluphenazine; clozapine; and others such as haloperidol.

- Mixed serotonin- and dopamine-blocking drugs: the new "atypical" class such as ziprasidone, risperidone, olanzapine, quetiapine, and aripiprazole.

Antidepressants—chemicals that make low moods less frequent by increasing energy or by decreasing anxiety. The main groups are:

- Serotonin reuptake inhibitors (SRIs): They change serotonin action by leaving it in the synapse for a longer time, which generally helps with anxiety. Examples are fluoxetine, sertraline, and citalopram.

- Norepinephrine reuptake inhibitors (NRIs): They change norepinephrine action in the same way SRIs affect serotonin, generally improving energy levels. An example available in the USA is bupropion.

- Mixed serotonin and norepinephrine reuptake inhibitors (NSRIs): Promote a balance, which can be more potent for some than either alone. Examples include venlafaxine and duloxetine.

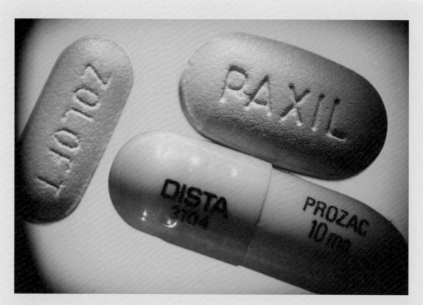

Figure 3.2 Paxil, Zoloft, and Prozac, three popular antidepressants. These medications are known as selective serotonin reuptake inhibitors (SSRIs) and are thought to beneficially increase the amount of serotonin in the brain. © *Leonard Lessin, FBPA/Photo Researchers, Inc.*

- Tricyclic antidepressants (TCAs): These usually act on both serotonin and norepinephrine reuptake sites, but may cause mild side effects. Examples include imipramine, desipramine and nortriptyline.

- Monoamine oxidase inhibitors (MAOIs): They slow an enzyme that breaks apart neurotransmitters. Examples include selegeline, tranylcypromine, and phenylzine.

Mood stabilizers—chemicals that prevent extreme mood swings.

- Lithium: Although still mysterious in how or how many ways it works, it does appear to boost serotonin activity and help to reduce impulsive behavior.

(continues)

(continued)

Figure 3.3 Lithium, a mood stabilizer that increases serotonin levels and controls impulsive behavior. © *GARO/PHANIE/Photo Researchers, Inc.*

- **Antiepilepsy medicines: They prevent excessive electro-chemical irritability in mood regions in the brain. They are prescribed even without true epilepsy, and include carba-mazepine, lamotigine, topiramate, and gabapentin.**

Sometimes a brief hospitalization can be very helpful for assessing and adjusting treatment daily, and should be considered well before suicide attempts occur. Suicidal thoughts merit careful attention at the very beginning, even if they do not contain suicidal intent at the outset. Sometimes they quietly grow to become wishes to self-harm in place of passive thoughts of not waking up. The slippery slope of incremental deepening of the darkness can bring thoughts that would never have been entertained at the outset. However, if a formed plan with suicidal intent is made clear, a therapist certainly must take action and is obligated to apply state laws (laws vary slightly from state to state). The therapist is then required to hold the person with or without the person's agreement. Billie-Jo's therapist had sensed that a change in the treatment might be needed because she seemed restless and more isolated, but she had believed that Billie-Jo would be able to call her if things got worse. Fortunately, Billie-Jo survived her overdose without a major problem. Now there was a dilemma. Because Billie-Jo had slept off the effects of the overdose, was it necessary for her to go to a hospital? There are several possible avenues in this kind of situation, including more frequent therapy visits, participation in an intensive outpatient program (day treatment), or a full inpatient stay for a week or two.

HELP WHEN SUICIDAL THINKING IS STRONG

After a long discussion with her therapist, Billie-Jo agreed that her feelings had been out of control for a while, and that she wasn't really safe. She understood some of the things that happen in the hospital with other people, like attending group therapy sessions and meeting individually with counselors or with a doctor at the hospital. Sometimes her outside therapist could visit, too. She could count on learning a lot about anxiety and depression there, how it happens, what it means, and also about how medicines help. Mental health problems should not be a cause for feeling shame.

Billie-Jo also learned about an enemy of healthy thinking, something that mental health professionals call cognitive rigidity. This means that most healthy people can usually change the way they think about problems when they feel stuck. The inpatient hospital group leaders teach ways to help build the flexibility—for example, by listening to the approaches others have used to solve similar problems.

Finally, Billie-Jo would also learn about some of the changes that occur in the brains of suicidal people. When she did enter the hospital, she saw that one doctor had framed on the wall a picture of scans of depressed, treated, and healthy people. After depressed people took medicines, their scans looked almost exactly like the scans of the healthy people, as if you could see the depression lift. She was curious about the scans, and asked the doctor to explain how the brain maps work. She understood that there are changes in activity levels in small areas of the brain in depression, and that they change with treatment. The doctor also explained that the activity maps were related to the amount of chemical reactions going on in the brain cells. Samples of spinal fluid, the fluid that surrounds the brain or brain tissue, taken after a completed suicide have been tested to see chemical changes related to suicide, but the information from the fluid is not useful for routine clinical care. The studies often have shown low concentrations of the breakdown products of the neurotransmitter serotonin, especially in people with both violent behavior and depression. In some of the studies, the measures would have almost had the power to predict suicidal behavior. The genes that control the activity of neurotransmitters, such as serotonin (discussed in Chapter 2: Impulses, Emotions, and Unexpected Behaviors), were clearly playing a key role in the regulation of mood. Environmental events were part of it, too, triggering the genetic vulnerabilities that affect the neurotransmitters.

Antidepressants affect the way serotonin works, and, not surprisingly, talk therapy affects serotonin activity in similar ways. There are real chemical changes that occur in depression, and they can change again for the better with treatment. The availability of better treatments and a greater variety of them is giving better results. One of the important next steps for researchers will be to find the best way to match individuals with the quickest and safest treatment.

Moods: Persisting, Swinging, and Distorting

"I have such terrible swings in my moods," Carla said. **"I had** them under control and stopped the medicine about six months ago because I was *sure* I was all better and that it wouldn't come back." Carla felt each of the rapidly changing feelings very deeply, causing her tremendous confusion because she could never predict how she would feel in the next hour, never mind tomorrow or next Saturday night. It took a few months for the benefits of the medicines to wear off. When they did wear off, the same exact feelings came back but now with a vengeance. Even her strong religious faith and connection to her family couldn't help her keep the thoughts and feelings away. With the old pattern returning, she tried to escape from becoming immobilized by the depression.

Carla wasn't sure what was driving all the ups and downs even though she worked very hard at thinking about all the possible causes. There was a guy pressuring her to go out with him, but he seemed to be interested more in kissing, petting, and sex than in knowing anything about her and the things she liked to do. Life seemed to be going faster and faster, with bad things happening to lots of kids her age. There was actually someone she had sort of known from school who had died while playing the choking game. She herself had never done that kind of thing, but it scared her that it was happening to people around her. The adults called it an accident, but really, the guy was gambling with his life, and he had boasted about it. She wasn't doing self-destructive things like cutting herself, drinking, or using drugs. She wasn't having sex just to be popular; she wasn't selling herself out. The ups and downs just came from nowhere. She couldn't figure it out.

DEPRESSION, PESSIMISM, AND MEDICINE

Mood illnesses are associated with about a third of all suicide attempts in adolescents[10] and up to half in the elderly.[11] When another primary problem is also present, such as substance abuse, anxiety, or posttraumatic stress disorder (PTSD), depression often complicates the situation. The good news is that depression (and the other problems, too) can get quite a bit better with treatment. Over 50 percent of people who suffer from depression get back to normal for reasonably long periods of months or years, although the risk remains that the depression will return. About 20 to 30 percent of adults with depression will only get somewhat better with the first efforts at treatment, and some of them may have more severe symptoms that cycle on and off for several years. This means that it can take an extra effort to beat the illness, using combinations of talk therapy, antidepressants, and boosters to help the first antidepressant work better. When the depression gets only partly better with an antidepressant medicine, the doctor sometimes will mix two types of antidepressant medicines, or might add a booster such as a thyroid supplement because a low thyroid level can indicate or contribute to depression. Also, new treatments are being developed all the time, making the future look brighter than ever.

Often, as in Carla's story, a part of the mood illness is to swing between extreme optimism and the bleakest pessimism. Extreme versions of this can be seen in bipolar disorder (having both ups and downs, also called manic depression). People with unipolar depression experience only the downs. In either illness, therapists try to teach patients to look at both the optimistic and the pessimistic viewpoints and try to find a compromise, otherwise the extremes may interfere with successful treatment. Especially in the early phases of an illness that results in a chronic recurrent depression, patients tend toward a pessimistic outlook and feel as if things will never get better. There is a tendency for people to get the wrong impression about their illness, thinking that things will be worse than they actually turn out to be.

Pessimism can peak in the early days of medication treatment before the benefits of the medication become apparent. This is a period of high suicide risk because the medicines are often started exactly at the time when there is a worsening of the illness. People often want immediate results, and it is frustrating

Bipolar Disorder

Bipolar disorder is characterized by periods of depression, sadness, and moments of deep hopelessness and rapid swings to an opposite mood state called mania. Mania causes wildly excited behavior with a very elevated mood, little need for sleep, and frequent spending sprees, among other risky behaviors. Other people don't get excited highs but get extremely irritable instead. At the onset of bipolar disorder, which usually occurs in childhood or adolescence, people are likely to experience only the episodes of depression. This can make it hard to tell depression and bipolar disorder apart for a long time, and many people with bipolar disorder may be treated for regular depression until the first episode of manic behavior surfaces. It is possible that treatment will not be fully effective until the diagnosis is clarified, and then treatments specifically designed for people with bipolar disorder can be started.

to have to wait two or three weeks to get a good response from the medication. Sometimes the medicines restore energy before the mood lifts. People with a pessimistic outlook may want to give up, and may be more dangerous to themselves if they have the energy to make a suicide attempt. Communication with a therapist and a doctor through this time is critically important, and once the response to the medication does kick in, very good treatment responses are common. If the first treatment trial doesn't work well, the wide range of continuously expanding treatment options means that no patient or therapist should ever give up a battle with depression.

Some patients who undergo treatment for depression begin to feel good again as a result of medication and are perhaps too hopeful in thinking that the good mood will be permanent. Most will decide, at least once or twice, that they no longer need their medication and stop taking it. This optimism is good and it shows that the medication is working well, but to stop medication suddenly and on your own is very unwise unless a mental health professional has been consulted. Carla took a big chance when she stopped her medication suddenly. Certain medicines should not be stopped abruptly because of a risk of seizures from withdrawal or because discontinuations can result in rapid declines in mood. Generally, discontinuation effects from stopping antidepressants are mild to moderate in severity, with low mood and body symptoms that resemble a flu-like illness (aches and pains, fatigue, stomach and intestinal problems, and discomfort in bright light). However, many people experience a sudden surge of depressive feelings and sometimes even suicidal thoughts after discontinuing antidepressants suddenly. The depression sometimes returns with greater severity than before, and is sometimes resistant to the medication treatments that worked before. Carla's symptoms came back after about six months, which makes it likely that this was a new episode of depression. Her attempt, shortly after restarting her medicine, came before the medicine was working well again. She might have avoided that new bout of depression—or at least made it much milder—if she had stayed on her medication.

It's important to watch people with depression when they suddenly seem to get better. A sudden change in mood might be a sign that the depressed person has made a suicide plan and has set a method, time, and place. Paradoxically, at these times, the depressed person might seem very happy. It is very difficult to detect when people have made these decisions unless they come forward and tell someone. To repeat a major point of this book: Communication is a major key to surviving with a severe depression.

DEPRESSION IS A CHEMICAL IMBALANCE

A fascinating demonstration of how brain chemistry can create negative thinking is seen in studies of depression where researchers observed the effects on mood by specially selected and prepared foods. Many aspects of nutrition and many chemicals in the brain are important and have effects on mood and brain function, but few are as specific as the effect of serotonin on mood. Around 1990 Dr. Pedro Delgado and his colleagues at Yale University conducted studies to learn how foods affect the activity of serotonin in the brain and can take control of moods. They were able to do this by creating special diets that excluded the part of food that is needed to make serotonin, an amino acid called tryptophan. In these studies, patients receive treatment with antidepressant medicines until they feel completely better, and then come to a research unit for a one-day diet test. The patients participated in the study twice in a double-blind experimental design, meaning that neither the patients nor the researchers knew if the active diet or a placebo (not active) diet was given on either day. In this way, researchers' judgments of a person's behavioral symptoms are not biased in one direction or another. By depriving research participants of tryptophan in the one-day diet, the levels of serotonin dropped rapidly in the brain, and researchers observed a dramatic return of depressive symptoms. The researchers measured tryptophan concentrations in the blood, and from other research, they knew that the serotonin levels in the brain are closely linked to the tryptophan

Suicide Predictors

Two things that can help prevent suicide are identifying and understanding factors that might precipitate increased risk, and factors that might be protective. A risk factor is anything that increases the likelihood that persons will harm themselves. However, risk factors are not necessarily causes. Research has identified the risk factors for suicide, some of which can be controlled to some extent:[12]

- previous suicide attempt(s)
- history of mental illness, particularly depression, and especially within the past year
- history of alcohol or substance abuse
- family history of suicide
- family history of child maltreatment
- feelings of hopelessness, perfectionism, or impulsive or aggressive tendencies
- loss (relational, social, work, or financial) or physical illness
- easy access to lethal methods
- barriers to mental health treatment
- isolation from other people

levels in the blood. Within a short time, the participants' mood became low and stayed low for about three hours. The stunning effect is believed to be due to the decline in brain serotonin, which is made from tryptophan. The results added convincing evidence that connected serotonin and depression, since the diet lacking tryptophan brought back the very same thoughts and behaviors that were observed in the patient before treatment

- unwillingness to seek help because of the stigma attached to mental health and substance abuse disorders or suicidal thoughts
- cultural and religious beliefs—for instance, the belief that suicide is a noble resolution of a personal dilemma
- local epidemics of suicide

Protective Factors

Protective factors buffer people from the risks associated with suicide. A number of protective factors have been identified:[13]

- effective clinical care for mental, physical, and substance abuse disorders
- easy access to a variety of clinical interventions and support for seeking help
- support from ongoing medical and mental health care relationships
- family and community support, including parental involvement in obtaining mental health care
- skills in problem solving, conflict resolution, and nonviolent handling of disputes
- cultural and religious beliefs that discourage suicide and support self-preservation instincts

for depression. The same worries returned, with the same self-blame, preoccupations, and even an identical slumped posture. During the evening after the test, the mood quickly returned to normal after regular food was given.

Patients who completed that study reported feeling convinced of the importance of chemistry in determining moods. Learning about the chemical basis of depression was empowering; it enabled them to regard their mood disorders as an illness and to stop blaming themselves for being depressed. Other more recent research has shown that brain functions are different during depression, and even more so during suicidal periods. Suicidal people *sound* different when they talk, which means that their brains are not controlling their voice normally. Sound engineers are developing ways to recognize the characteristic voice changes, so that someday the volunteers who listen to crisis hotline calls may have some help in deciding when to be especially forceful in urging callers to go to the hospital.

Mood disorders are one of the major causes of suicide, so it is important to know what and why our moods are what they are. Negative situations or events make us sad, but sometimes these things get overemphasized and become self-fulfilling. For example, Carla noticed that when she was depressed, she tended to look down at the sidewalk on her way home. She never saw her friends waving to her from across the street. When she felt better, she felt much more comfortable looking at people's faces when speaking to them, took time to look at the flowers and the sky, and didn't pay too much attention to unpleasant things around her. Carla's friends wondered why she suddenly would seem very upset about a small issue, but then didn't show any excitement about major positive events. When people feel bad, they sometimes become convinced that something bad has happened, and will even look for things that are wrong. A balanced view is needed, seeing both good and bad together. With depression, the mind sees negative things in detail but has more difficulty appreciating the positives, even if they're abundant. If you saw a white room while wearing regular sunglasses, you would believe that it is actually a green room. Depression tints the world gloomy. Treatment often quite literally brings dramatic changes. Patients will say, "I didn't know that colors could be so strong and exciting."

COMMUNICATION AS A PRIORITY, A THERAPY GOAL

Today's busy lifestyles can interfere with quality family time. Carla's parents were very busy professionals who planned family time together but would often be called away, even in the middle of a board game. Her family all had good communication skills, but there wasn't time to practice them, and energy was exhausted on activities at work and school. When the family talked about their situation in therapy sessions, it was apparent that they weren't really spending quality time together. Carla could see that she wasn't connected to people anymore, and she blamed herself for not being more successful, for not earning more attention, and for not fitting in at school. She had never before needed to express her needs verbally, since her parents and siblings had always been there, almost magically knowing what would please her and make her feel loved. No one noticed what was happening because everyone's time and energy were directed elsewhere.

Shared features in most types of talk therapies include the development of communication skills, the dedication of attention and support, and the expectation that both the patient and the therapist will bring energy to the session. Carla's therapist, Dee, seemed to always be in the same mood, even smiling when she told Carla to work harder at being on time. That became an example of learning communication skills. Carla talked about heavy traffic, having to drive her brother to soccer practice, and then having difficulty finding parking near Dee's clinic. Dee calmly asked if there had been any discussion of these problems

Changes Measured in Brain Research That May Indicate Suicide Risk

Suicides in older people are associated with several illnesses that damage the brain. In certain types of brain scans it is quite common to see special features, a few small spots called *hyper-intensities* or, sometimes, *unidentified bright objects* (UBOs), especially in people over 50 years old. It has been shown that even in young adults, having a lot of these spots in the presence of depression is associated with a larger number of suicide attempts prior to the brain scan.[14] In theory, the spots might be places where critical pathways or circuits in the brain are disrupted. When there is a problem with blood circulation in the brain, a part of the brain does not receive enough oxygen and can become damaged. The spots might be a result of brain damage from poor blood flow caused by prior suicide attempts; or it may be that the spots were present prior to the attempt and might cause suicidal thinking to be more frequent and intense. Therefore, it is important to discover if the causes of these UBOs precede the suicide attempts. Finding the cause(s) of UBOs might point to ways to prevent them, and then maybe we could prevent the development of some of the high-risk suicidal thinking patterns in the brain.

Multiple sclerosis (MS, a disease of the fibers that connect brain circuits),[15] certain treatments for Parkinson's disease[16] (a disease of nerve cells that make an important chemical at home. Carla slowly realized that solving her problem with timeliness was in and of itself a form of therapy. She'd have to find the right way, at the right time, to communicate with her

called dopamine), and early Alzheimer's disease[17] (a disease that damages memory and mood centers) are often associated with suicide risk. They all cause fatigue or disability, but other illnesses with similar amounts of fatigue and disability don't seem to cause as many suicide attempts. Depression is common in people with MS, Parkinson's disease, and Alzheimer's disease. The depression seems to be specifically related to the brain damage from each of these illnesses.[18] For example, it has been reported that when MS strikes only spinal cord fibers and not the brain, it causes less depression. This and other types of evidence give researchers reason to believe that brain damage to specific areas causes depression and suicide.

Certain other illnesses also cause depression and suicide attempts, and researchers believe that these can be caused by blood-borne factors secreted by other parts of the body. These factors appear to reach the brain, cause changes in brain function, and lead to suicidal thoughts and behavior. For example, any form of lung disease almost doubles the normal risk of suicidal thoughts or behavior. Gastrointestinal ulcers increase the risk by about one-third, and AIDS (acquired immunodeficiency syndrome) increases the risk about 44-fold, even when any preexisting emotional problem is taken into account. An unexplained, first episode of depression in an older person should prompt a checkup for pancreatic cancer, which is rare, but that can show its first sign as unexplained depression.

parents and ask them for their suggestions. She would need to have the energy to communicate well.

Progress in problem solving was slow because Carla's mood swings seemed to get in the way. She had resumed medication and it was starting to help, but a mix of worry, shame, insignificance, hopelessness, helplessness, and anger would well up and get in the way when she thought about talking with her parents. When she finally discussed the timeliness problem with them, the driving routines were fixed in only two minutes of talking. It had taken four weeks to drum up the courage, and it was good to have it done, but it was also frustrating to think of the difficulty she had just getting through that first piece of therapy homework. Fortunately, Dee had been patient with her. Carla started thinking that maybe being a bit calmer about things would make communication easier.

After a while, the therapy seemed to be working, even though Carla felt suspicious and wasn't counting on it lasting a long time. Her disappointment with the recurrence of the mood swings was painful. She talked with Dee about her fear that her depression would come back, and they worked on recognizing early signs, and how to fight them. For one thing, if her sleep patterns were disturbed, the risk would increase. Keeping the same bedtime, even on weekends, would be worthwhile if it would help her keep the depression and irritability from returning.

Carla learned to recognize other warnings by reviewing her journal entries. When she wrote too many "they" and "them" words, she might be feeling separated from people, and more time and energy on communication would be worthwhile.

A third warning was her memory playing tricks on her. When she felt down and alone, it was hard to remember good things. She practiced retrieving special, good memories, especially some moments that had really felt loving. She learned that she could work on the overly persistent, nagging thoughts and her mood swings, which took self-awareness, knowledge of ways to shift her moods, and lots of energy and time.

Recognition of these warning signs was helpful for Carla. Similar techniques work for other people, too. Researchers have found that specific parts of the brain "light up" when people try to recall emotional experiences. These areas, called the frontal lobes, mostly in the front of the brain, are also involved in processing memories, especially emotional memories. Talk therapy or medication, or the two together, seem to help the frontal lobes to work more normally. Carla is on track to build a good life for herself.

Living with
Being "Different"

David was struggling with two big issues that made him feel *very different from the other kids in school. He wasn't having sexual feelings toward girls the way other guys seemed to but was realizing that he felt attracted to other boys. He knew that this didn't mean he had to be gay, but he was starting to feel that the attraction was real and that it wouldn't go away just because other people said it would. He had one close friend, a girl he'd known for about 10 years, but it was not romantic at all, and they always talked about clothes and shopping. He was rather obsessed with style and neatness. His parents were very rigid about most things and he couldn't imagine them accepting him if they knew he were gay. It was all on his mind much more since his friend, Erica, had asked him to a dance and when he'd said no, her feelings seemed hurt. She asked if he were gay. He told her that he wasn't sure. She seemed angry, and they didn't talk for several days until he told her that he missed talking and hoped that they could stay friends. She seemed happy to get back to the familiar, chatty conversations with him. He worried, however, that someday another boy would ask her out and he'd be out of luck.*

David had been receiving or giving himself shots for his diabetes every day since he was four years old, which restricted his ability to spend time away from home. He couldn't go on the weeklong hunting and camping trips with his brother and father. His mom watched him like a hawk, always checking to see if he had tested his blood sugar every day. She was pretty anxious herself. He believed that her nervousness started when he was diagnosed.

At times David felt as if his situation was so hopeless that suicide seemed to be the only way to manage it all. One day while chatting with Erica, he decided to tell her about his plan. For a long time, they had shared their private thoughts about feeling alone, even in their families. Sometimes David had told her that he didn't feel understood or wanted by his parents, and he had said that sometimes he just wanted to never wake up. Erica made him promise to tell her beforehand if he were thinking about hurting himself. She had pleaded with him not to leave her alone. He had promised. In retrospect, talking with Erica had saved his life. She had made it clear—either she would call for help or he would make an appointment right there in front of her. Her reaction was calm but firm. She made clear that since she cared about him she couldn't let anything bad happen to him.

David was hopeful that therapy would help. Coping with everything was something he would need to learn about, and he knew it would take time. He knew his problems would work out in the long run, but just thinking about them would stop him for days at a time, and he didn't feel that great the rest of the time. His angry outbursts at his mother made him feel guilty, and he even felt guilty because he was sure that she was feeling guilty, too. She had never let it slip, but he was sure she blamed herself deep down for his diabetes although the doctors said it was a random happening, like a roll of the dice.

When he spoke with the therapist, his thoughts about suicide were still coming up, but he was already getting better at pushing them away. He promised to call her if they seemed to be getting worse. He said he wanted to try to work things out, even if the cost of therapy made him feel more guilt. He felt a sense of guilt and hopelessness at least half of the time. The therapist asked about his sleep, which was lousy and he was always tired. It was hard to get *things done or concentrate on anything. His appetite and energy had never been very good with the diabetes, but they were worse now, and sometimes his blood sugars were too low. She also asked about interests in and out of school, and he realized that this had changed, too. He was just dragging through each day, his grades were falling, and he wasn't even as excited as usual about the new fashions for the season. He thought she was clairvoyant when she asked about feelings of worthlessness, which bothered him even more than the hopelessness. He usually could convince himself that there would be hope somewhere, but he could never shake the feeling that he was a burden and a disappointment to his family. She said that she wasn't clairvoyant at all, but that it was a thought pattern that was common among people with depression. The depression, she explained, was causing these symptoms on its own, bringing up things that weren't true, and then repeating them over and over. He felt stuck but at least he wasn't alone, since her being there when he talked about it all seemed to help a lot.*

SUICIDE IN GAY, LESBIAN, BISEXUAL, AND TRANSGENDERED YOUTH

Since the late 1980s, there has been more attention in the mainstream treatment community given to the social problems faced by lesbian, gay, bisexual, or transgendered (LGBT) individuals. This coincided with heightened urgency to counsel people about the spread of HIV and drug abuse, especially among gay men, and has begun to produce better treatment of the needs of young LGBT individuals trying to cope in a heterosexual world. In 2005 Drs. Kimberly Balsam, Theodore Beauchaine, Ruth Mickey, and Esther Rothblum reported results from a very large survey that showed that LGBT adolescents are at higher risk for suicidal behavior.[19] Comparing LGBT teens to their heterosexual siblings revealed that a LGBT sexual orientation was associated with greater **suicidal ideation** (or actively

thinking about suicide), suicide attempts, self-injurious behavior, the use of psychotherapy, and the use of psychiatric medications. The findings regarding the mental health of LGBT
individuals remained true even after taking into account factors
of family adjustment. The heterosexual siblings, however, were
just as likely as the LGBT group to report current psychological
distress, psychiatric hospitalizations, and low self-esteem.

Evidence suggests that suicide risk is increased when a person shows personality traits associated with the opposite sex.
Gender roles should be discussed as part of risk assessments.
Advocates suggest that schools should be proactive in providing
counseling. Helping LGBT students retain a sense of empower-
ment may help avert suicide, alcohol and other drug abuse, and
homelessness, all of which are cited as greater risks in this group.
The turmoil of coming out and being rejected by one's parents
appears to be especially difficult for LGBT individuals who
show what might be considered "feminine" personality traits.
The suicide attempts of these individuals met with less forgiv-
ing and empathic attitudes from their peers than the suicide
attempts following diagnosis of an incurable illness, suggesting
that social isolation from peers can add to the stress of estrange-
ment in the family unit at this difficult time.

David apparently had suicidal feelings due to both the
prospect of coming out and due to his grades slipping. Erica's
response—first anger, later empathy—might be typical of peer
responses. She initially showed indifference to his suffering about
the sexual identity problems due to her lack of knowledge and
discomfort, but respected his struggle with the long-standing
diabetes and the new problems with failing quizzes and tests.

CHRONIC ILLNESS AND SUICIDE

The tension at David's house surrounding his diabetes had
become part of the routine—an uncomfortable but familiar

elephant in the room that everyone was used to and never talked about. There would be a major change in his relationship with his mother when he went to college and she had to trust him to do his routine care independently. He already knew that she'd be counting the days and would be able to tell by the syringe refills whether he was keeping up. He was annoyed, felt trapped, and had urges to "do something" but he had no idea how to let out his feelings of frustration.

His therapist had been working with adolescents with chronic medical conditions for some time and said that these feelings of frustration are not uncommon in these situations. She also said that the feelings can be expressed, and she hoped they would be in a constructive way. She gave him some statistics about the relationship between having a chronic illness and expressing frustration by doing unhealthy or dangerous things. One might expect that the presence of a chronic illness could make the average adolescent more cautious or timid, but the opposite usually appears to be true. About 10 percent of more than 3,000 adolescents reported a chronic illness on an 80-question survey from a 2003 study from Switzerland.[20] Their responses were compared to their healthy peers. Both the boys and girls with illnesses were more likely to report current tobacco use, more alcohol use, and were less likely to wear seatbelts than their healthy counterparts. More boys with chronic conditions had used cannabis than other boys, while the girls with chronic illness were more likely to have driven while drunk in the prior 12 months. The percentage of students who had made suicide attempts in the prior 12 months more than doubled in the presence of a chronic illness in both the boys and the girls.

The therapist proposed alternatives to David, suggesting that he spend more time playing his flute and maybe try to get some lessons at the local conservatory. She said that having a chronic illness and having more frequent contact with medical doctors

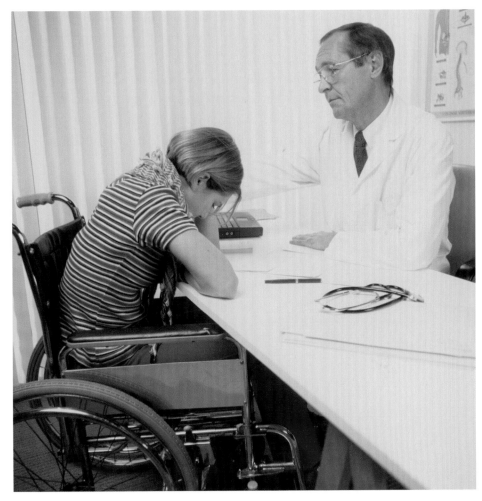

Figure 5.1 A woman is comforted by her doctor. The loneliness and hopelessness experienced by those with chronic illnesses or disabilities can lead to suicidal behavior. © *CC Studio/Photo Researchers, Inc.*

wasn't the same as getting psychological attention for the difficulties that young people with illnesses face. The same group of Swiss researchers found that almost 15 percent of teens 15 to 20 years old had at some time made a suicide plan, and 3 percent reported past suicide attempts. Even though about 50 percent of the two groups (the group that had attempted suicide and the non-attempt group) had seen a physician, only 10 percent of those who had made attempts had spoken with the physician about the attempt. This is again a wake-up call to the medical community, suggesting that current interviewing methods are not successful enough in detecting suicidal thoughts in adolescents. Once again, communication through the early phases of stressful events is key.

Suicide, Risk Factors, the Brain, and Treatments

We've just seen several examples of regular people suddenly finding themselves in a difficult emotional situation, and how decisions made in that state of mind can have overwhelming consequences. Suicidal thoughts and behavior are very old problems. They have been described in ancient writings, including the Bible.[21] The feelings are not part of our imagination. The fact that they have been around for thousands of years suggests that something goes awry in the wiring of the brain. This chapter will discuss, in a more general way, the findings from research about suicide and possible treatments.

RISK FACTORS FOR SUICIDE

People who suffer from a mental disorder may not have exactly the same symptoms as someone else with the same illness. When the symptoms are sufficiently similar, they can be grouped to form useful definitions of mental disorders.

Emotional symptoms and illnesses are major risk factors for suicide in young people. For example, depressive symptoms in a major depressive disorder raise the risk of suicide almost fivefold. The same or greater risk occurs in people with bipolar disorder who have manic highs that alternate with depression. It surprises people that suicidal individuals do not always have depression as their basic problem. For example, a group of people with what are called *disruptive disorders* (where they

Table 6.1 Factors That Increase the Risk for Suicide[22]

SLIGHT RISK: LESS THAN 3-FOLD	MODERATE RISK: MORE THAN 3-FOLD, LESS THAN 8-FOLD	STRONG RISK: MORE THAN 8-FOLD, LESS THAN 15-FOLD	VERY STRONG RISK: MORE THAN 20-FOLD
Low self-worth*	Depression	Disruptive disorders	Prior suicide attempts
Low socioeconomic status*	Infrequent support from parents*	High distress over sexual abuse in boys	AIDS
Loneliness	Infrequent support from peers*	Bipolar disorder**	
	Parents' excessive drinking	High body mass index**	
	High distress over sexual abuse in girls		
	Perception of academic failure		

*Factors associated with more frequent hospitalizations
** Factors requiring further study

frequently show disruptive behavior in social situations) have an increased risk of suicidal thoughts or behaviors by almost a factor of 10.[23] Table 6.1 lists a number of risk factors. The more risk factors present, the higher the risk.

Besides depression and mania, many other emotional symptoms may arise in response to stress in the environment. Even though depression is not always present, suicidal thoughts *do* precede almost all suicide attempts: More than 90 percent of attempters recall suicidal ideation prior to an attempt.[24] How can we understand suicide when people have so many different stresses in their lives and each person has individual reactions to those stresses?

Researchers working on understanding stress have tried to develop scales that measure how much stress an event might

Occurrences: Statistics

- The myth that there is a link between the winter holidays and suicides is not supported by several surveys that suggest that rates are lowest in the winter and highest in the spring.[25] Additional data are needed to assess whether treatments, including the increased use of light box therapies for seasonal affective disorder and newer antidepressants, has had an effect on winter and spring rates.

- Suicide took the lives of 30,622 people in 2001 in the United States.[26] The number was 31,647 for 2004, giving age-adjusted rates that remain statistically steady at about 10.7 to 10.8 deaths per 100,000 persons per year for each of the most recently reported years, 2003–2004.[27]

- At the time of final editing of this book, many individual states have posted data for 2005. Some states provide narrative reports that are helpful in understanding the circumstances surrounding these deaths. Communication about distress is key. For example, a 2005 Oklahoma report reviewed deaths of teens and found that only 13 percent of them were seeing a counselor at the time of the death. Also, only 17 percent had a prior attempt, so an absence of prior attempts is not very reassuring. Conflict with parents was present in 44 percent, while substance abuse was present in 22 percent. One teen death was attributed to a lost pet.[28]

- Suicide rates 10 years ago were generally higher than the national average in the western states and lower in the eastern and midwestern states.[29]

- In 2002, 132,353 individuals were hospitalized following suicide attempts; 116,639 were treated in emergency rooms and released.[30]

cause. Even positive events, like a wedding or a child's birth, are stressful. There is less known, though, about the relative weight of different kinds of stress for children and adolescents. Similarly, less is known about risk factors for suicide in children and adolescents than for adults, but slowly this is beginning to change as researchers have more opportunities to talk with young people who are suicidal.

Researchers have found that some of the risk factors that have been found in adults are also likely to affect children and adolescents. Repetition of a suicide attempt within a year appears to be four times more likely if the person is engaging in drug or alcohol abuse. Repetition of an attempt is also four times more likely if someone has severe problems with separating reality from fantasy (delusions or hallucinations) that are not part of depression or mania. Chronic medical conditions or illnesses or a history of sexual abuse also brought a threefold increase in the risk of a repeat attempt within a year.

Past sexual abuse often causes lasting hopelessness and depression, which are risk factors for suicidal behavior. Some 55 percent of boys and 29 percent of girls who were sexually abused will attempt suicide, and these rates are tragically significant because sexual abuse remains a persistent and distressingly not uncommon event.[31] Sexual abuse can lead to suicide even without causing depression first: Being upset by abuse doesn't always show up as depression. For example, some people may suddenly decide to attempt suicide rather than face the embarrassment of talking about the abuse they experienced. This means that it's not enough just to watch out for depression to stop suicides. Stopping sexual abuse is a high priority from every point of view, and it will also be helpful in lowering suicide rates.

SPECIAL RISK FACTORS FOR ADOLESCENTS

Although overdose is the most common means of suicide attempt,[32] the prescription of antidepressants appears to decrease suicide attempt rates.[33] When multiple risk factors are present together, they have much more than simply additive effects on attempt rates.[34] Lethality is predicted by a prior attempt history, so that even with assurances that "it will never happen again," strong monitoring for recurrences of suicidal thought is advised. Disputes or relationship breakups are risk factors and have brought on attempts in more than three-fourths of the histories.[35] Another large percentage of adolescents who attempt suicide have a history of a prior mental health evaluations resulting in diagnoses of depression or depressed mood (77 percent), or drug or alcohol abuse (19 percent), so that these also indicate potentially additional risk.[36]

Knowing about these risk factors has helped to focus outreach efforts, but it has not been enough to make a major change in the rates of suicide attempts. Most of the risk factors are actually quite common, as discussed in Abe's story, which makes it very difficult to identify individuals who are in danger of committing suicide unless the person informs someone directly about a suicide plan.

A study published in 2005 reported on about 400 people with mood disorders who were followed prospectively for 40 years. Over 10 percent died by suicide during that period.[37] Depression was most lethal early in the illness, and the suicide rate declined through the lifetimes of the patients. (Based on this data, this is another reason to wait out the illness in adolescence, since things seem to get better with time.) Being in the early phases of a depressive illness is a major risk factor, and early therapeutic interventions are critical for the prevention of suicide. There was a significant benefit to those who remained

Risks Differ For Different People

Males

- Suicide is the eighth leading cause of death for all U.S. men.[38]

- Males are four times more likely to die from suicide than females.[39]

- Suicide rates are highest among white men and second highest among Native Americans, including those in Alaska.[40]

- Of the 24,672 suicide deaths reported among men in 2001, 60 percent involved the use of a firearm.[41]

Females

- Women report attempting suicide during their lifetime about three times as often as men.[42]

Adults

- For men and women combined, the percentage of suicides by firearms was 55 percent in 2003 and 52 percent in 2004.[43]

Youth

- The overall rate of suicide among youth has declined slowly since 1992 according to a report from the Centers for Disease Control and Prevention.[44] However, rates remain unacceptably high. Adolescents and young adults often experience stress, confusion, and depression triggered by situations occurring in their families, schools, and communities. Stress triggers many illnesses, including mental illness. Such feelings can overwhelm young people and lead them to consider suicide as a solution. Stress is sometimes used as an excuse, as a way of minimizing

Teen deaths by suffocation rise

Hanging and suffocation have overtaken guns as the chief means of suicide among Americans 10 to 14 years old, according to a recent government study.

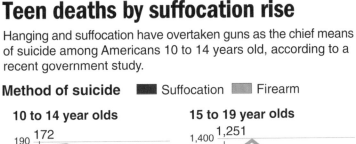

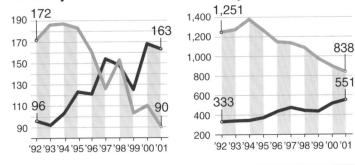

SOURCE: Centers for Disease Control and Prevention   AP

Figure 6.1 Graphic illustrating the decline in use of guns and the rise in suffocation and hanging as means of teen suicide. © *AP Images*

the importance of depressive symptoms. Removing the stress does not cure the heart of the damage it has done, nor does depression lift when stress is lighter. Depression causes more stress. Depression studies show the need for better methods for systematic detection. Few schools and communities have suicide prevention plans that include screening, referral, and crisis intervention programs for youth, but schools in some areas are beginning to put such programs into place.

- The online TeenScreen program, sponsored by Columbia University, uses a 10-minute questionnaire called the

(continues)

(continued)

Columbia Health Screen, which can be provided through school systems. The Web site has won awards, but others object to having this sort of screening associated with school records or even with the teachers who grade the students. Another objection is that the number of children who would be unnecessarily referred for follow-up assessment often squeezes the capacity of most community mental health systems, so that valuable resources might be pulled away from individuals who are at greatest risk.

- Suicide is the third leading cause of death among young people ages 10 to 14 and also 15 to 24. The ranking of suicide in causes of death rises rapidly as early childhood illnesses become less common. The rate for children of latency age (5 to 9 years old) is about 50 times lower than for early teens (10 to 14 years old). In 2001 3,971 suicides were reported in this group.[45] The estimated number in 2004 was 4,214, or 10.1 per 100,000 persons, and remains the third leading cause of death, following accidental and homicide deaths. Cancer was a distant fourth, at 4 per 100,000 for persons 15–24 years of age. Suicide rates remained even higher in other age groups, with the highest among the elderly.[46]

- Of the total number of suicides among those ages 15 to 24 in 2001, 86 percent (n=3,409) were male and 14 percent (n=562) were female.[47]

- Native Americans, including those in Alaska, had the highest rate of suicide in the 15 to 24 age group.[48]

- In 2001, firearms were used in 54 percent of youth suicides.[49]

The Elderly

- Suicide rates increase with age and are very high among those 65 years and older, although suicide at this age is no longer among the top 10 causes of death. Most elderly suicide victims are seen by their primary care provider a few weeks prior to their suicide attempt and diagnosed with their first episode of mild to moderate depression. Older adults who are suicidal are also more likely to be suffering from physical illnesses and be divorced or widowed.[50]

- In 2001, 5,393 Americans over age 65 committed suicide. Of those, 85 percent (n=4,589) were men and 15 percent (n=804) were women. Firearms were used in 73 percent of suicides committed by adults over the age of 65 in 2001.[51]

active in treating their illness, both in terms of measurement of quality of life and longevity.

Emergency room doctors only get to see people who come in with intense suicidal thoughts and those who survive their attempts. Are there risk factors that predict the medical severity of an attempt? Unfortunately, no such risk factors have been identified so far. The usual risk factors cannot predict whether an attempt will be lethal. We can hope that younger adolescents will make fewer lethal attempts but, unfortunately, younger individuals seem to make attempts that are often highly lethal. First attempts can be extremely lethal, often occurring before individuals seek help for hopelessness or depression.[52] The adolescent years can bring marked isolation and secret distress. More and more Web sites and counselors have been made available for adolescents and have helped to prevent suicides, but even more outreach is needed.

BRAIN INJURY AS A RISK FACTOR

Some of the risk factors for suicide have taught neurobiological researchers about areas in the brain that seem to be involved in suicidal behaviors. People who have experienced injuries to certain parts of the brain, and not so much for other parts, seem to be at higher risk for suicidal thoughts and other poorly controlled impulse behaviors. By studying these injuries, we are able to learn more about where suicidal thoughts come from.

In addition, accidents are more likely to occur to people who are impulsive, aggressive, or hostile. These traits are also risk factors for suicide even without brain injury. To try to understand whether the brain injury or the accident-prone traits bring on suicide attempts, researchers listed the methods used in suicide attempts by an impulsive group and a brain-injured group.[53] They found that brain-injured individuals use the same methods in attempts as noninjured impulsive people. The injuries do not seem to change the type of behavior, but might increase the amount of suicidal behavior.

To study this further, the researchers divided people who had attempted suicide into two groups—those with or without brain injury before the attempt. The group with prior brain injuries had more males with histories of substance abuse, aggression, and hostility than the group without brain injuries. Attempts were mostly predicted by aggression and hostility, and not by the presence of brain injury.[54] It remains possible that mild brain damage in childhood (from falls or other common events) could cause impulsive behavior, and brain injury later in life due to impulsive behavior could increase suicide risk. It is also possible that genetic predispositions might cause risky and impulsive behaviors that lead to both brain damage and suicide attempts. Whichever is the "original" problem,

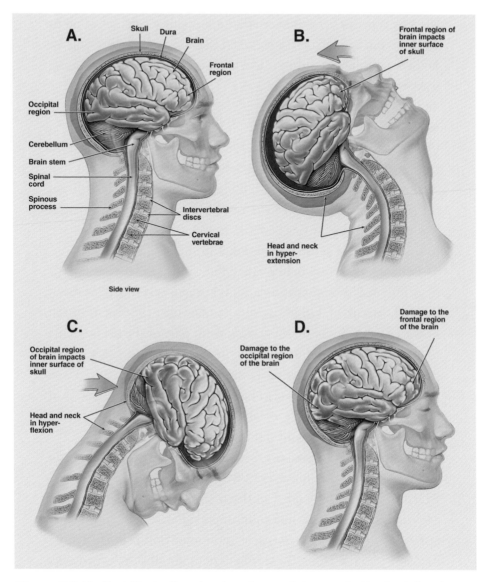

Figure 6.2 Medical illustration showing stages of damage to the frontal and occipital (rear) regions of the brain. Brain damage can be linked to suicidal behavior. © *Nucleus Medical Art/Visuals Unlimited.*

the cycle between increasing damage and increasing difficulty in controlling behavior needs to be addressed in treatment. Each additional risk factor makes an individual more prone to suicide. Why these particular risk factors cause suicides remains unclear, but understanding their effects on the brain will be helpful for understanding causes of suicide and finding better ways to prevent it.

WHAT HAPPENS IN THE BRAIN?

Once someone is prone to suicide by having one or more risk factors, what and where are the actual changes in the brain that initiate suicidal thoughts? Are there specific parts of the brain that repeatedly show up in the results of studies about suicide? Are physical injuries or chemical changes in these parts of the brain believed to cause depression and suicidal behavior?

Doctors began to believe that the brain was the source of emotions and thoughts about 200 years ago, and much has been learned since then. For example, a stroke (interruption of blood flow to part of the brain) in the *left* front part of the brain seems to cause depression, but a stroke in the *right* front part of the brain seems to cause mania (extreme elevated mood). Certain other brain illnesses may also have associations with depression and suicide. The balance of activity in the brain hemispheres seems important in mood stability.

What is it that throws off this balance in the brains of young people who become suicidal but who haven't had brain damage? Exactly what has happened in the brain? Many clues have been explored, and it is a bit like collecting evidence at a complicated crime scene with many possible molecular and cellular actors, mediators, and victims. To summarize many studies, depression and suicidal behaviors are associated with changes in the frontal cortex, amygdala, anterior thalamus, hippocampus, ventral striatum, brainstem, and certain structures that connect these areas together. Depression, suicide, and aggressive and impulsive behaviors are also associated with changes in the workings of certain brain chemicals called neurotransmitters. The changes in specific neurotransmitters cause changes in the activity of these brain regions, and vice versa. It is considered likely that problems in one or more of the neurotransmitters and brain regions are triggers for depression and suicidal behavior, but since they're all working in a network, it is unlikely that there will be a single cause of these problems that affects everyone in the same way.

TREATMENTS: RISKS AND BENEFITS

Treatments help most people feel at least partly better within a few weeks. Thoughts of suicide should become less frequent, less intense, and briefer when they do come up. All types of treatment involve the active participation of the patient. It is important to encourage depressed and suicidal people to continue treatment, even when the illness saps their motivation or there is a delay in feeling the benefits of the treatment. Treatments slowly help people to help themselves by learning to bring back positive feelings. Treatments do not replace a person's own will, make people change in a predetermined way, or force people to do new things. Guidance from a therapist can help people identify their problems and find their own answers, so that they can assert their self-control.

Treatments help suicidal people once the person agrees to come for help. This is probably the greatest hurdle to overcome: getting treatment to the right people at the right time. There's a sort of paradox here. Depression causes low self-esteem, and many people who have low self-esteem are less likely to ask for help because they feel that they're "not worth it" or that asking for help means that they're weak or crazy. Actually if someone feels low self-esteem and depressed, especially if suicidal thoughts are occurring, it takes bravery and strength to ask for help. Depression changes people's thinking so they believe the illness is their fault, they think they don't deserve treatment, they believe that no one else could possibly understand how they feel, and they become too ashamed to ask for help. At some point, these people no longer have the depression—it's the depression that has *them* and is doing the thinking for them.

The biological basis of mental illness has been known for many years, but most people still don't understand that these illnesses are like having an invisible broken leg. Mental illnesses are not imaginary or fake—we can see the changes in many types of brain scans and measurements of brain activity and chemistry. They are not caused by faulty personal decisions and they are not punishments for bad behavior. It is very important for people to talk about emotional problems rather than hiding them.

Treatments do help people get through periods of depression and help control suicidal thoughts. Additionally, treatment may help people recognize changes in their lifestyles that may precede depression, such as changes in sleep patterns, new stressful events, exercising less than usual, or changes in diet.

Suicide is still far too common. Why is this? How effective are our current treatments? How do they work? Is it possible for a treatment to become a risk factor for suicide?

The last of these questions has received a great deal of media and scientific attention recently. At the same time as these concerns may be causing decreased utilization of treatments available for depression, data from 2004 collected by the U.S. Centers for Disease Control and Prevention (CDC) and reported in the February 2007 issue of the medical journal *Pediatrics* show an increase in death rates for children in only one category, which is called "intentional self-harm (suicide)."[55] While a causal relationship has not been proven, it is equally of concern that undertreatment of depression may result in increased suicide risk, especially given the sizeable (15 percent) increase in the death rate for 10- to 19-year-olds from 5.3 in 2003 to 6.1 per 100,000 in 2004. Discussions about the risks and side effects of antide-pressants themselves became more frequent beginning in 2003. The controversy is not new, dating back to the earliest use of medications that affect the mind, including all anesthetic agents and certainly all street drugs. One concern is that medicines for the treatment of depression might accidentally trigger a worsen-ing of symptoms, possibly even lead to a suicide attempt in some young people. As of 2006, very highly controversial interpreta-tions of data had been compiled from many different treatment studies. Mixing the different studies makes conclusions difficult to assess. At this writing, the best available evidence supports the conclusion that treatments for depression themselves are *not* causes of worsening depression or suicide. Rather, the onset of depression and suicidal thoughts are reasons to start treatment, so it is not surprising that there are suicidal behaviors observed at the beginning of treatment. Still, any time a medication affects the brain, there is a possibility that the effects might be good for one person and bad for another. Since everyone is just a little dif-ferent from everyone else, we can only make a prediction of how each individual will respond based on the observations of many other people in research studies.

Research studies are conducted with the best ethical inten-tions by the pharmaceutical industry, with tremendous moni-toring efforts by the U.S. Food and Drug Administration, all at enormous cost. There is always room for improvement, and improvements are always sought in the design and man-agement of the trials. The pharmaceutical industry already tries to use research study designs that can accurately detect rare events such as suicide and whether they are caused by the drugs or by the illness. The use of placebo comparisons in these studies remains an important strategy for testing for adverse effects of the active study drug. Any rare event, though, will remain difficult to test for statistical significance unless study populations become much larger, and unless pharmaceutical trial study populations include more subjects who report suicidal thoughts at the beginning of the study. These subjects are excluded from almost all trials because of the increased suicide risk for them in participating in research, but it means that the studies are based on subjects with less suicidal versions of depression. These efforts will receive greater scrutiny in the future.

Also, the doctors who prescribe the medicines are becoming more insistent on combining such treatment with talk therapy. The caution raised by some of this new data emphasizes the need for careful, frequent monitoring of medications and their possible side effects from the start of treatment.

Researchers will continue to try to determine whether anti-depressants bring any added risk, whether the risk is shifted from one small group of depressed people to another small group, how to minimize any detectable added risk, and whether there is a way to predict who will get bad side effects from any given medication. The side effect of having new suicidal thoughts is uncommon and is believed to affect, at most, a very small number of people who take the medicines. It is possible that such side effects might occur when medicines change brain chemicals or regional activities in ways that are similar to the effects of the brain illnesses discussed above, but there is no credible proof that this is true. It has been repeatedly shown that very few suicide attempts occur in people who are taking their medicines; the postmortem toxicology tests usually can tell when a medicine is taken regularly and is processed by the body, as opposed to showing only the unprocessed medicines that are detected after an overdose.

No matter how good the medications are, this controversy will continue to be fueled by a healthy public skepticism of the pharmaceutical industry, so we can assume that it will be an ongoing question. In the meantime, whatever might be believed to be the cause of suicidal thoughts, communication and safety are critically important. If starting new medication causes a difficult transition, but the medication saves lives in the long run, it seems to be worth the effort to monitor patients carefully at the beginning and during a change in treatment. This should be considered good medical practice, even without the controversy about medication side effects.

Medications for any illness that are suspected in rare instances to cause an increased risk of depression and suicide should be used only if clearly needed and then with great caution. Old medications for high blood pressure (reserpine and beta-blockers) and relatively new medicines for multiple sclerosis or viral hepatitis (interferon) or for acne (isotretoin) have been suspected in numerous reports, and some of the evidence is of considerable concern to scientists. None of these medicines has been absolutely proven to cause depression or suicide, but once under suspicion, it is very difficult to prove them to be absolutely safe. Reserpine is now rarely used because of this concern and because safer medicines can be used instead. When equally helpful medicines are not available and a suspect medicine is chosen for use, the doctor should discuss these potential risks with patients and their families. Doctors and families need to be extra careful to watch out for, and treat, depression or suicidal thinking if it does occur while using these medicines, but no one should stop taking medications without consulting his or her doctor.

WHICH MEDICINES ARE BEST?

A large number of antidepressant treatments are available for patients with depression. These treatments can be applied with or without the presence of suicidal thoughts. Treatments for depression need to be used more carefully in people who also have had manic behavior in the past because of greater risks of sudden mood changes—possible switches into a manic episode—during treatment. There are also many treatments for bipolar disorder, but they differ considerably from treatments for other forms of depression. Some family physicians or general practitioners prefer to ask for consultation from a psychiatrist for their patients with bipolar disorder.

How do antidepressant medicines work, and how do such simple chemicals change our moods? The first group of antidepressant medications, the monoamine oxidase inhibitors (MAOIs) were developed in a span of about 10 years beginning in the late 1950s. The second generation, called tricyclic antidepressants, are still used as a second-line approach today because they are very effective. These medicines are usually not the first to be tried because side effects of some of them, such as fatigue, weight gain, dry mouth, blurry vision, and constipation, are quite bothersome even at moderate doses.

More recent versions of those first medicines and the newer families of antidepressant medicines (**serotonin reuptake inhibitors [SRIs]**, and also a group called heterocyclics) have fewer side effects. The controversy discussed above is mostly focused on the SRIs. (See Chapter 3 for more information on the SRIs and other medications.) Overall, the treatments definitely do work: In that same 40-year follow-up study described in the beginning of this chapter, it was clearly shown that lithium, tranquilizers, and antidepressants reduced suicide deaths significantly; that long-term treatment gave lower overall mortality (deaths from all causes); and that combined treatments (talk therapy with medication) were most effective.

CHALLENGES IN BRAIN RESEARCH

To understand how antidepressants and talk therapies work, it is important to understand what goes wrong in depression and suicide in the first place. This is difficult because the brain is extremely complex and difficult to study because it is wrapped in bone, many parts are far from the surface, and all the parts are different from one another.

Researchers can see that there is a very complex network of axons (the long arms of brain cells that reach out to one another), capillaries (the blood supply), and synapses (the small gaps between the ends of axons and the next brain cell, where there are connections). We can see that messages are moving around because when they are active, the axons change shape, the synapses change the electrical properties of the outer cell membranes, and the capillaries bring more food and carry away more waste. What we do not understand is why the messages choose certain pathways at a specific time, or which pathways are exactly linked with which thoughts.

This research is still a work in progress. Scientists have found many markers of changes in the brain that are associated with depression or suicidal thinking, but it has not been possible to catch the initial causes of all of those changes. Genetics, stress in childhood, and other factors are believed to interact in important ways to cause the changes that are seen in the brains of people with depression and suicidal thoughts. Like traffic in a large city, changes in the brain are hard to track because the system doesn't have a single clear "downstream" pathway. The brain has a complicated network, so every event can potentially trigger hundreds of other changes, and the changes that are seen could just be consequences of a problem elsewhere, and not truly original causes of the whole problem. Also, most of the known changes are only seen in certain subtypes of depression. None appears to be universal.

In addition to the complexity of the brain, depression is complex, too. It comes in almost as many subtypes as there are flavors of ice cream at the local ice cream shop. There are different treatments for the different subtypes, so it is important for the doctor to understand which kind of depression has occurred. For example, a subtype of depression called **melancholia** (Latin *melan* for "black" and *choli* for "bile") is a particularly dark form that brings changes in daily rhythms of appetite, sleep, and mood, and is associated with abnormally regulated, excessive release of natural steroids in the body. Melancholic depressions are likely to be quite responsive to certain new antidepressants, the older tricyclic antidepressants, and **electroconvulsive therapy (ECT)**, probably more so than other subtypes of depression. It can be very important that the doctor recognizes the melancholic subtype of depression when it is present because it is a severe form of depression that carries very great risk. ECT is generally reserved for adults with extremely severe, life-threatening illness. There are several other kinds of depression, including atypical depression (which is probably a misnomer, since it appears to be a common type). Atypical depression causes low, blue feelings that are not very different from the sadness people feel when someone dies. Atypical depression brings on the opposite changes in appetite and sleep patterns from those seen with melancholia. Instead of causing a decrease in sleepiness and appetite as seen in melancholia, both of these behaviors are increased, causing weight gain and daytime napping. This subtype often responds well to other classes of antidepressants, such as the SRIs, NSRIs, or MAOIs (described in Chapter 3). Table 6.2 gives some examples of these differences, but it should be understood that none of these generalizations is perfect. Both types of depression are very serious, and both can be treated.

RESEARCH ON SUBTYPES OF DEPRESSION

Some of the research from the past 10 years is showing that there are specific molecules that are only affected in certain subtypes

Table 6.2 Comparison of the Symptoms of Melancholia and Atypical Depression

MELANCHOLIA	ATYPICAL DEPRESSION
Insomnia	Excessive sleep
Poor appetite and weight loss	Excessive appetite, weight gain
Slow movements, picking at clothing	Vigilance, awareness of surroundings
Low morning mood, brighter in afternoon	Often worse in evening, but not necessarily; less regular mood changes
Avoidance of social contact	Worse when alone
Highly lethal suicide attempts	Frequent lower-risk attempts, yielding a high risk in long run

of depression. This is important because in most studies that find a marker of depression, the marker isn't present in all of the depressed people, and it might be seen in some of the healthy people at the same time. So none of these markers is perfectly matched to a diagnosis. No single change appears to be present in all people with depression or suicidal thoughts.

Starting in the mid-1990s, researchers began to measure certain communicator proteins in brain cells called *second messengers* that also appear in skin cells. When a neurotransmitter binds to the receptor on the cell surface, second-messenger proteins are sent to the center of the cell where these proteins help to switch on and off many of the genes that keep the cell active and replace worn out parts. Studies of these proteins and their role in various subsets of depression reveal those people with melancholic depression have different results from people with other forms of depression and from **healthy controls.** Healthy controls are people without depression or illness who participate in a research study of a new medicine or treatment process; the people's behavior and response to the medicine or process serves as a comparison to that of participants with depression or illness. The melancholic patients showed a specific problem in the communication proteins that go between the receptors on the cell surface and nucleus.[56] The change in the protein is present all the time, and appears to be a risk factor for melancholia. The change doesn't seem to cause problems as long as the nerve cell doesn't have to grow or learn new tricks. This may indicate that melancholia emerges in people when they are stressed or exposed to new conditions. If there is too much change, the nerve cell can't keep up because the communication within the cell isn't working correctly. The communication that these special proteins bring to the nucleus has an effect on many of the genes that control the whole brain cell, including the formation of the special proteins themselves.

The research has shown dramatic differences between melancholia and other depression subtypes that will someday help us understand melancholia, how our current treatments work, and how they might be made better. The work strongly supports the hypothesis, which most researchers believe to be true, that genetics may put some people at greater risk for melancholic depression.

Another new area of research looks into the brain as a moving machine, and studies how it changes over time. These studies first examined variability in heart rate starting in the mid-1990s. In the early years of this century, studies of variability in brain chemistry, and also in brain activity maps, have been published. Instead of taking the average of many single snapshots of chemical or activity profiles, this research method looks at how patterns of the chemical levels or activities change from one moment to the next. The studies suggest that there is less variability in the heart rate, the brain chemistry, and the activity levels of people who are depressed. It appears that the brain is changing its normal patterns more slowly in depression, just like the moods themselves seem to change more slowly. Finding the reason for the slow chemical changes may be helpful in understanding depression, and also in understanding how antidepressants work.

These studies and many others are promising and may someday explain the basic problems in the brain that lead to depression and suicidal thinking. Once we have those answers, it will be easier to figure out exactly how antidepressant medications and talk therapies may make the basic problem of depression go away.

TYPES OF TALK THERAPY

Talk therapy should always be a primary part of treatment for people who are or have ever been suicidal. Even with the best of medicines, the risk of side effects will always be greater than the risk of talk therapy, and the benefits appear to be about the same for most people with mild to moderate depression, as long as suicidal thoughts are not occurring. The differences appear to come in the short-term costs and ease of use, and possibly also in people with very severe depressions for whom the combination of medication with talk therapy appear to have a clear advantage.

Talk therapies need to be customized for each patient, and a trained pyschotherapist should be able to recommend the best treatment. For example, patients with multiple sclerosis (MS), a severe disease of the nervous system, sometimes get depressed. Fortunately, for most of them it seems that their depression gets better with almost any type of therapy. If the first treatment doesn't work, many doctors will choose a specific type of medical treatment that helps even those still depressed after one treatment trial. This specific treatment for

Do Some Medicines Increase Suicide Risks in Young People?

Some medicines may have risks, but more research is needed to be sure. Fortunately, most adolescents are healthy and don't require many medications. Research remains relatively scarce on these issues. Moods are adversely affected by very many medicines. The controversy about SRIs is not at all settled.

Numerous articles have addressed this controversial problem, with no definitive answers since each has examined the problem differently. An editorial in the *British Medical Journal* summed up several related papers and concluded that evidence of benefits of SRI prescription in adolescents is outweighed by these risks, and that in the absence of sufficient knowledge of the effects of these medications on the developing brain (it is thought that it slows down its development at about age 20), the routine use of SRIs in adolescents should be discouraged.[57] An opposite view, published in the *American Journal of Psychiatry*, expressed a defense of these medications, and noted that increases in prescriptions for SRIs have paralleled overall lower suicide rates over time, and also that SRIs are less lethal in overdose than the older tricyclic family of medications.[58] Some of this mixture of opinions may be better understood by examining individual reports on the subject.

Another article in the *British Medical Journal* studied data from several hundred research trials sponsored by pharmaceutical companies and found a weak indication that SRIs may be associated with more self-harm behaviors than placebo, but no significant effect on overall deaths.[59] A study published in the *Acta Psychiatrica Scandinavica* examined 14,857 suicides and found that SRI antidepressants were less likely to be associated with suicide than other, non-SRI antidepressants.[60] However, this is difficult to interpret because SRIs are frequently used as first line treatment in populations for whom their cost is affordable, whereas individuals who don't get better with SRI treatment, can't afford SRIs, and or have chronic illnesses that are more frequently treated with less expensive, non-SRI antidepressants such as tricyclics are susceptible to greater illness severity. This might explain the larger proportion of suicides with the other antidepressants.

Yet another article in the *British Medical Journal* examined a combined data set that totaled 87,650 participants in 702 trials and found that suicide attempts were about two times more frequent with SRI antidepressants than placebo (odds ratio 2.28) or non-antidepressant therapies (odds ratio 1.94). However, there was no difference in the rates of completed suicides among the treatments.[61]

At the time this book goes to press, the question will not have been resolved overall. It remains likely that most individuals will benefit from SRI prescriptions. However, virtually all of these articles, including those with positive findings, urge early follow-up assessment after an antidepressant prescription is given. (The author recommends that since antidepressant medications have powerful effects on mood and other brain activities, they should be used in the context of talking psychotherapies. Most often, medications have beneficial effects, but this cannot be assured with current diagnostic criteria for all who might receive them. Medication effects can be seen as *permissive;* they allow you to feel good if you are doing things that are enjoyable. They are not automatic "uppers." Talking psychotherapy offers several major benefits in the combined

(continues)

(continued)

treatment strategy: it is as good in many patients (but not all) as medications alone; it offers the patient assistance in developing new positive understandings of life opportunities; and it offers more frequent monitoring of mood changes that occur during treatment.)

Another publication found that younger children, ages 5 to 14, had lower suicide rates in counties that had greater numbers of antidepressant prescriptions for the years 1996 to 1998. This research approach was made more promising and potentially meaningful by adjustments that accounted for differences among counties in distributions by gender, race, income, and mental health care availability.[62] However, suicide is very uncommon in preteen children, and similar data for adolescents from age 15 to 19 who have sixfold higher suicide rates than the younger cohort will be needed to assuage concerns about effects of these medications on suicide risk in the older adolescent.

Psychiatric side effects will affect about 5 percent of people taking a corticosteroid. Most of these side effects will be mood problems, and even with slow tapering of these medications, there is often a new set of mood-related side effects when they are stopped.

A study of acne medicines, which adolescents use relatively frequently, evaluated brain scans to see if different acne treatments cause changes associated with suicidal behavior.[63] Isotretinoin, a medicine commonly given to adolescents to treat acne, decreased brain activity by about one-fifth in the orbitofrontal cortex, but no change was seen during treatment with a common antibiotic. This area of the brain is known to mediate symptoms of depression. Unfortunately, it is not currently possible to predict who might be vulnerable to these depressions, and it is difficult to prove whether any of these side effects are truly a result of the medicines.

severe depression in MS patients is to use desipramine, one of the tricyclic antidepressants along with therapy that focuses on coping skills.

For people with suicidal thoughts, many types of talk therapies are available. Some of the most common are interpersonal psychotherapy (IPT), psychodynamic psychotherapy, supportive therapy, and cognitive-behavioral therapy (CBT). Recently, many treatment centers are offering dialectical behavior therapy (DBT), which is a kind of CBT, for people with more chronic illnesses. Studies, including some large studies published in 2005, have shown that if people are treated with CBT, subsequent self-harm is less likely than if regular, nonspecific treatments are given. It should be noted that some experts have criticized CBT research studies because the academic centers that run them have therapists with very advanced training. So, if a less-adept therapist tries to practice CBT without this advanced level of training, a patient might not find it as effective.

Most therapists specialize in certain types of therapy, and will recommend one of the therapies they use most. Usually, this is a reasonable approach. If it does not work well, however, it may be worthwhile to look for a therapist who is specifically trained in the use of CBT or in IPT, both of which are highly successful methods. Dialectical behavior therapy (DBT) is also recently gaining greater recognition. The bottom line is, if it's working, continue, and if it's not working after a reasonable trial period, then it's probably time to try a change. Therapists should be able to help patients find the best form of therapy for them.

Research shows that suicide is less likely with treatment in a maximally supportive clinical environment, even for high-risk patients. The supportive environment might mean being admitted to a hospital, but it would be well worth the time, expense, and possible humiliation—giving up a week or two in the hospital to save the next 50 or so years of life and learn how to make those years much better. Periods of suicide risk can be very brief and can come without warning, so a hospital stay should be strongly considered for people with active suicidal thoughts, even if specific suicidal plans are not present. Suicidal ideation can come suddenly, and might last only a few minutes or hours, so that mental health professionals are not able to completely predict suicide attempts.[64] A supportive, safe, communication-friendly environment—in a therapy setting or in a hospital—should be made always available as an option.

In addition to talk therapy, many people with depression are also prescribed antidepressants. The current trend of using medications that have fewer side effects has led more people to take these medicines than ever before. People with mild depression, including some with even less severe symptoms, are being treated more with medication and less with therapy, even though there is not enough research to document that benefits outweigh risks of medication use in these relatively mild conditions. People often choose medicines because they are easy to obtain, cost less in the short run (but possibly much more in the long run than a brief course of CBT), and do not require time off work for weekly 45-minute sessions. Also, therapy sessions can be hard work, requiring attention, focus, and disclosure. They aren't all about "feeling good"—it's actually more like schoolwork, requiring a fair amount of concentration, and often even homework. Disclosure—telling one's secrets—is hard for many people. These and other factors have led to an increase in medication use.

Medication risks are small and not often serious, but when so many people are taking them, even the slight risk of infrequent but severe side effects becomes a problem. Talk therapy has virtually no risks or side effects. In individual (one-on-one) therapy, talking about personal secrets is hard, even though it is extremely rare and usually illegal for a certified therapist to release confidential information. Even in group therapy, where people worry that confidential material might leave the therapy setting, it has been shown that breaches of confidence are very unlikely to occur. In view of these issues, better suicide prevention will require an improved availability of qualified therapists, better management of financial costs for the patient, and public acceptance of the time and effort commitment required for therapy.

CONCLUSION

Even though researchers don't know exactly what goes wrong in every depressed or suicidal brain, much has been learned recently and the future is brighter than ever. Research trials of new treatments continue to be highly promising.

New treatments are exciting, but the first hurdle is often the hardest: communication is key. *Not* getting help when things are getting crazy prevents even the best research results from having a chance to work. People—both those trying to get help and those wanting to give it—need to communicate better. Most suicides, about 70 percent, occur within 30 days of a visit to a physician, and one estimate suggests that 50 percent occur in the first week. Some things are not being said (82 percent do not communicate their intentions to the physician), and what is said isn't always heard. A study about 50 years ago suggested that most suicides had been preceded by a warning to relatives or friends, and, on average, to three people within that year. This sounds very insufficient, but many others *are* heard, and treatment prevents the attempt and reduces the suicidal symptoms. Those statistics are harder to collect, but we know that around one out of five people have a serious episode of depression at least once in their lives.

There are now many ways to tell if a specific talk therapy or antidepressant is actually helping. Study methods have been refined over the past few decades, and continue to be improved so that more and better treatments can be safely developed. One thing is absolutely clear: With more treatment options becoming available every year, no one should ever give up hope.

1. R.C. Kessler et al., "Prevalence, Severity, and Comorbidity of 12-month DSM-IV Disorders in the National Comorbidity Survey Replication," *Archives of General Psychiatry* 62, no. 6 (June 2005): 617–27.

2. D.L. Foley et al., "Proximal Psychiatric Risk Factors for Suicidality in Youth: The Great Smoky Mountains Study," *Archives of General Psychiatry* 63, no. 9 (September 2006): 1017–24.

3. J.A. Yesavage and V.O. Leirer, "Hangover Effects on Aircraft Pilots 14 Hours After Alcohol Ingestion: A Preliminary Report," *American Journal of Psychiatry* 143, no. 12 (December 1986): 1546–50.

4. Keith A. King, "Fifteen Prevalent Myths Concerning Adolescent Suicide," *Journal of School Health* 69, no. 4 (1999): 159–60.

5. H.A. Bergen et al., "Sexual Abuse and Suicidal Behavior: A Model Constructed From a Large Community Sample of Adolescents," *Journal of the American Academy of Child and Adolescent Psychiatry* 42, no. 11 (2003): 1301–9; H.A. Bergen et al., "Sexual Abuse and Suicidality: Gender Differences in a Large Community Sample of Adolescents," *Child Abuse and Neglect* 28, no. 5 (2004): 491–503.

6. A. Caspi et al., "Influence of Life Stress on Depression: Moderation by a Polymorphism in the 5-HTT Gene," *Science* 301, no. 5631 (July 18, 2003): 386–9.

7. A.R. Hariri et al., "Serotonin Transporter Genetic Variation and the Response of the Human Amygdale," *Science* 297, no. 5580 (July 19, 2002): 400–3.

8. F. Bellivier et al., "Association Between the TPH Gene A218C Polymorphism and Suicidal Behavior: A Meta-Analysis." *American Journal of Medical Genetics: Part B Neuropsychiatric Genetics* 124, no. 1 (January 1, 2004): 87–91; D. Rujescu et al., "Genetic Variations in Tryptophan Hydroxylase in Suicidal Behavior: Analysis and Meta-analysis," *Biological Psychiatry* 54, no. 4, (August 15, 2003): 465–73; P.Y. Lin and G. Tsai, "Association Between Serotonin Transporter Gene Promoter Polymorphism and Suicide: Results of a Meta-Analysis," *Biological Psychiatry* 55, no. 10 (May 15, 2004): 1023–30; M. Anguelova, C. Benkelfat, and G. Turecki, "A Systematic Review of Association Studies Investigating Genes Coding For Serotonin Receptors and the Serotonin Transporter: II. Suicidal Behavior," *Molecular Psychiatry* 8, no. 7 (July 2003): 646–53; P. Courtet et al., "Suicidal Behavior: Relationship Between Phenotype and Serotonergic Genotype," *American Journal of Medical Genetics C: Seminars in Medical Genetics* 133, no. 1 (February 15, 2005): 25–33; P.F. Courtet et al., "The Monoamine Oxidase A Gene May Influence the Means Used in Suicide Attempts," *Psychiatric Genetics* 15, no. 3 (2005): 189–93.

9. G.K. Brown et al., "The Internal Struggle Between the Wish to Die and the Wish to Live: A Risk Factor for Suicide," *American Journal of*

Psychiatry 162, no. 10 (October 2005): 1977–9.

10. See note 2 above.

11. Y. Conwell, P.R. Duberstein, and E.D. Caine, "Risk Factors for Suicide in Later Life," *Biological Psychiatry* 52, no. 3 (August 1, 2002): 193–204.

12. U.S. Public Health Service, *The Surgeon General's Call To Action To Prevent Suicide.* (Washington, DC: Department of Health and Human Services, 1999). Available online. URL: http://www.surgeongeneral. gov/library/calltoaction/default.htm. Accessed June 6, 2007.

13. Ibid.

14. E. P. Ahearn et al., "MRI Correlates of Suicide Attempt History in Unipolar Depression," *Biological Psychiatry* 50, no. 4 (2001): 266–70; S. Ehrlich et al., "White Matter Hyperintensities and their Association with Suicidality in Depressed Young Adults," *Journal of Affective Disorders* 86, nos. 2–3 (2005): 281–87; S. Ehrlich et al., "White Matter Hyperintensities and their Association with Suicidality in Psychiatrically Hospitalized Children and Adolescents," *Journal of the American Academy of Child and Adolescent Psychiatry* 43, no. 6 (2004): 770–76; S. Ehrlich et al., "Subanalysis of the Location of White Matter Hyperintensities and their Association with Suicidality in Children and Youth," *Annals of the New York Academy of Sciences* 1008 (2003): 265–68.

15. R.J. Siegert and D.A. Abernethy, "Depression in Multiple Sclerosis: a Review," *Journal of Neurology, Neurosurgery, and Psychiatry* 76, no. 4 (2005): 469–75.

16. S. Takeshita et al., "Effect of Subthalamic Stimulation on Mood State in Parkinson's Disease: Evaluation of Previous Facts and Problems," *Neurosurgical Review* 28, no. 3 (July 2005): 179–86

17. W.S. Lim et al., "Early-Stage Alzheimer Disease Represents Increased Suicidal Risk in relation to Later Stages," *Alzheimer Disease and Associated Disorders* 19, no.4 (October–December 2005): 214–9.

18. P. Gareri, P. De Fazio, and G. De Sarro. "Neuropharmacology of Depression in Aging and Age-Related Diseases," *Ageing Research Review* 1, no. 1 (February 2002): 113–34.

19. K.F. Balsam et al., "Mental Health of Lesbian, Gay, Bisexual, and Heterosexual Siblings: Effects of Gender, Sexual Orientation, and Family," *Journal of Abnormal Psychology* 114, no. 3 (August 2005): 471–6.

20. L. Miauton, F. Narring, and P.A. Michaud, "Chronic Illness, Life Style and Emotional Health in Adolescence: Results of a Cross-Sectional Survey on the Health of 15- to 20-Year-olds in Switzerland," *European Journal of Pediatrics* 62, no. 10 (October 2003): 682–9.

21. H.J. Koch, "Suicides and Suicide Ideation in the Bible: An Empirical Survey," *Acta Psychiatrica Scandinavica* 112, no. 3 (2005): 167–72.

22. A.S. Richardson et al., "Perceived Academic Performance

as an Indicator of Risk of Attempted Suicide in Young Adolescents," *Archives of Suicide Research* 9, no. 2 (2005): 163–76; T.P. Sokero et al., "Suicidal Ideation and Attempts Among Psychiatric Patients with Major Depressive Disorder," *Journal of Clinical Psychiatry* 64, no. 9 (2003): 1094–1100; H.A. Bergen et al., "Sexual Abuse and Suicidal Behavior: A Model Constructed From a Large Community Sample of Adolescents," *Journal of the American Academy of Child and Adolescent Psychiatry* 42, no. 11 (2003): 1301–9; B. Groholt et al., "Young Suicide Attempters: A Comparison Between a Clinical and an Epidemiological Sample," *Journal of the American Academy of Child and Adolescent Psychiatry* 39, no. 7 (2000): 868–75; A.S. Richardson et al., "Perceived Academic Performance as an Indicator of Risk of Attempted Suicide in Young Adolescents," *Archives of Suicide Research* 9, no. 2 (2005): 163–76.

23. See note 2 above.

24. Marianne Wyder and Diego De Leo, "Behind Impulsive Suicide Attempts: Indications from a Community Study," *Journal of Affective Disorders*, In Press, Corrected Proof, available online. URL: http://www.sciencedirect.com/science/article/B6T2X-4NCKJBS-1/2/bd22cc8ec77403c4fbdecd0f4de49ae6. Accessed June 7, 2007.

25. Centers for Disease Control and Prevention, National Center for Injury Prevention and Control. "Suicide Surveillance, 1970–1980." (1985); R. McCleary et al., "Age-and

Sec-Specific Cycles in United States Suicides, 1973–1985," *American Journal of Public Health* 81 (1991): 1494–7; C.W. Warren, J.C. Smith, and C.W. Tyler, "Seasonal Variation in Suicide and Homicide: A Question of Consistency," *Journal of Biosocial Sciences* 15 (1983): 349–56.

26. Centers for Disease Control and Prevention, National Center for Injury Prevention and Control (producer). Web-based Injury Statistics Query and Reporting System (WISQARS) [online]. (2004) Available online. URL: http://www.cdc.gov/ncipc/wisqars. Accessed June 21, 2004.

27. A.M. Miniño, M.P. Heron, and B.L. Smith, "Deaths: Preliminary data for 2004," *National Vital Statistics Reports* 54, no. 19 (June 28, 2006): 4.

28. Oklahoma Child Death Review Board, *2005 Annual Report.* Available online. URL: http://okcdrb.ouhsc.edu/pages/2005Report.pdf. Accessed November 25, 2006.

29. Centers for Disease Control and Prevention, "Regional Variations in Suicide Rates—United States 1990–1994," *Morbidity and Mortality Weekly Report* 46, no. 34 (1997): 789–92. Available online. URL: http://www.cdc.gov/mmwr/preview/mmwrhtml/00049117.htm. Accessed June 6, 2007.

30. See note 26 above.

31. H.A. Bergen et al., "Sexual Abuse and Suicidality: Gender Differences in a Large Community Sample of Adolescents," *Child Abuse and Neglect* 28, no. 5 (2004): 491–503.

32. D. Safer, "Self-Reported Suicide Attempts by Adolescents," *Annals of Clinical Psychiatry* 9, no. 4 (1997): 263–9.

33. O.W. Morgan, C. Griffiths, and A. Majeed, "Association Between Mortality from Suicide in England and Antidepressant Prescribing: An Ecological Study," *BMC Public Health* 4 (December 21, 2004): 63.

34. N. Garnefski and R.R. Diekstra, "Suicidal Behavior and the Co-occurrence of Behavioral, Emotional and Cognitive Problems Among Adolescents," *Archives of Suicide Research* (1995). Available online. URL: http://www.priory.com/adsui2. htm. Accessed April 12, 2007.

35. S.A. Kidd and M.J. Kral, "Suicide and Prostitution Among Street Youth: A Qualitative Analysis," *Adolescence* 37, no. 146 (Summer 2002): 411–30.

36. D. Shaw, J.R. Fernandes, and C. Rao, "Suicide in Children and Adolescents: A 10-Year Retrospective Review," *American Journal of Forensic Medicine and Pathology* 26, no. 4 (December 2005): 309–15.

37. J.Angst et al., "Suicide in 406 Mood-Disorder Patients With and Without Long-term Medication: A 40 to 44 Years' Follow-up," *Archives of Suicide Research* 9, no. 3 (2005): 279–300.38. R.N. Anderson and B. L. Smith, "Deaths: Leading Causes for 2001," *National Vital Statistics Report* 52, no. 9 (2003): 1–86.

38. R.N. Anderson and B. L. Smith, "Deaths: leading causes for 2001," *National Vital Statistics Report* 52, no. 9 (2003): 1–86.

39. See note 26 above.

40. See note 26 above.

41. See note 38 above.

42. E.G. Krug et al., eds., *World Report on Violence and Health* (Geneva: World Health Organization, 2002). Available online. URL: http://www.who.int/violence_injury_prevention/violence/world_report/en. Accessed June 6, 2007.

43. See note 27 above.

44. K.M. Lubell et al., "Methods of Suicide Among Persons Aged 10–19 years—United States, 1992–2001," *Morbidity and Mortality Weekly Report* 53 (2004): 471–73. Available online. URL: http://www.cdc.gov/mmwr/PDF/wk/mm5322.pdf. Accessed June 7, 2007.

45. See note 38 above.

46. See note 27 above.

47. See note 38 above.

48. See note 26 above.

49. See note 38 above.

50. See note 12 above; S.S. Carney et al., "Suicide over 60: the San Diego study," *Journal of American Geriatric Society* 42 (1994): 174–80; T.L. Dorpat, W. F. Anderson, and H. S. Ripley, "The Relationship of Physical Illness to Suicide," in *Suicide Behaviors: Diagnosis and Management,* H.P. Resnik, ed. (Boston: Little, Brown, and Co., 1968).

51. See note 26 above.

52. M.H. Swahn and L. B. Potter, "Factors Associated With the Medical Severity of Suicide Attempts in Youths and Young Adults," *Suicide and Life-Threatening Behavior* 32, no. 1 (2001): 21–29.

53 M.A. Oquendo et al., "Suicidal Behavior and Mild Traumatic Brain Injury in Major Depression," *Journal of Nervous and Mental Disease* 192, no. 6 (2004): 430–434.

54. Ibid.

55. B.E. Hamilton et al., "Annual Summary of Vital Statistics: 2005," *Pediatrics* 119, no. 2 (February 2007): 345–60.

56. D. Akin et al., "Signal Transduction Abnormalities in Melancholic Depression," *International Journal of Neuropsychopharmacology* 8, no.1 (March 2005): 5–16.

57. A. Cipriani, C. Barbui, and J.R. Geddes, "Suicide, Depression, and Antidepressants," *British Medical Journal* 330, no. 7488 (February 19, 2005): 373–4.

58. R.D. Gibbons et al., "The Relationship Between Antidepressant Medication Use and Rate of Suicide," *Archives of General Psychiatry* 62, no. 2 (February 2005): 165–72; R.D. Gibbons et al., "The Relationship Between Antidepressant Prescription Rates and Rate of Early Adolescent Suicide," *American Journal of Psychiatry* 163, no. 11 (November 2006): 1898–904.

59. D. Gunnell, J. Saperia, and D. Ashby, "Selective Serotonin Reuptake Inhibitors (SSRIs) and Suicide in Adults: Meta-Analysis of Drug Company Data from Placebo Controlled, Randomized Controlled Trials Submitted to the MHRA's Safety Review," *British Medical Journal* 330, no. 7488 (February 19, 2005): 385.

60 G. Isacsson, P. Holmgren, and J. Ahlner, "Selective Serotonin Reuptake Inhibitor Antidepressants and the Risk of Suicide: a Controlled Forensic Database Study of 14,857 Suicides," *Acta Psychiatrica Scandinavica* 111, no. 4 (April 2005): 286–90.

61. D. Fergusson et al., "Association Between Suicide Attempts and Selective Serotonin Reuptake Inhibitors: Systematic Review of Randomised Controlled Trials," *British Medical Journal* 330, no. 7488 (February 19, 2005): 396.

62. R.D. Gibbons et al., "The Relationship Between Antidepressant Prescription Rates and Rate of Early Adolescent Suicide," *American Journal of Psychiatry* 163, no.11 (November 2006): 1898–904.

63. J.D. Bremner et al., "Functional Brain Imaging Alterations in Acne Patients Treated with Isotretinoin," *American Journal of Psychiatry* 162, no. 5 (2005): 983–91.

64. A. Fagiolini et al., "Suicide Attempts and Ideation in Patients with Bipolar I Disorder," *Journal of Clinical Psychiatry* 65, 4 (2004): 509–14.

GLOSSARY

abstain, abstinence—Total cessation of an activity, usually referring to the use of drugs or alcohol. Exposure to sufficient levels of addictive substances often leads to serious dependency problems. Rates of addiction after self-exposure are related to brain mechanisms affected by each drug. Alcohol and drug usage causes brain diseases. Refraining totally from alcohol and substance use is considered best for relapse prevention and recovery.

amygdala—A small almond-sized brain region just below and behind the eyes that controls behaviors such as mood, anxiety, and anger.

antidepressant medications—Medications used to treat depression, anxiety and panic disorders, bipolar disorder, and many other illnesses. They are divided into three major classes, with subtypes also available: antidepressants, tranquilizers, and mood stabilizers. An example of the first is the selective serotonin reuptake inhibitors (SRIs; for example, generics fluoxetine, paroxetine, sertraline); benzodiazepines (antianxiety medications, for example, generic alzaprazolam); and mood stabilizers (for example, lithium, a naturally occurring salt that is used to treat bipolar disorder).

anxiety disorder—Anxiety disorder is an illness that can be measured with imaging scans and other scientific tools. There are many effective treatments that can relieve the symptoms of anxiety. Stress from anxiety is considered a risk factor for heart disease, and has been associated with poor healing from infections, surgeries, and cancer. Anxiety disorders can lead to symptoms of depression, and vice versa. Depression and anxiety together create a higher risk for suicide than either of them alone.

bipolar disorder—In this relatively common disorder, mood swings are uncontrollable and severe. There are subtypes being researched recently that show a continuum of moods (irritable, high, or depressed) in severity. Many very famous and successful people had this disorder, and modern treatments can usually help prevent the symptoms from remaining severe for long periods of time. Even though it was called manic depression not too long ago, most patients have much more of the depression than the mania. People with this disorder should seek help to maintain their mental health.

chromosome—One of 46 large pieces of genetic material, each containing (on average) about 1,000 genes. Chromosomes are shaped like the letter X. They can be distinguished from one another by their size and patterns of bands on their arms. In males, one of the chromosomes is shaped like a letter Y. Chromosome 17, which holds the SLC6A4 gene that is discussed in the text, and most of the other chromosomes come in pairs, so that one variant copy of a gene does not necessarily cause a problem.

control—A person without depression or illness participating in a research study of a new medicine or treatment process; the person's behavior and response to the medicine or process serves as a comparison to that of a person with depression or illness.

depression—Depressed people have depressed moods (feeling sad, blue, or down in the dumps) or losses of interest in usually pleasurable hobbies or activities, or both. Many will show some of the following signs as well: extremes in appetite, sleep patterns, energy or activity levels, and difficulty concentrating on tasks. They often feel excessively guilty, hopeless, or worthless. Any one or two of these problems can occur without a diagnosis of serious depression, but if several of the symptoms are present, there is at least cause for seeking help.

Atypical depression is a common disorder (regardless of its name) that causes low, blue feelings that are not very different from the sadness people feel when someone dies.

diagnosis—The diagnosis of emotional illnesses is based on symptoms that are reported by the patient and family, family history of emotional illness, and other factors. There are currently no absolute tests that objectively prove the presence of a diagnosis, but doctors agree on most diagnoses for an individual with very high levels of certainty. When a diagnosis is in doubt, however, it is possible that time can sometimes show that the first diagnosis was incorrect, or that more than one diagnosis should have been made. The diagnosis helps doctors decide what kind of talk therapy, medication, and therapist to recommend See also **talk therapy.**

electroconvulsive therapy (ECT)—A medical treatment for extremely depressed adults who do not respond to medication or talk therapy; the induction of electrical waves that relieves the severity of depression for adults who have severe, melancholic depression.

functional magnetic resonance imaging—Pictures of brain structures can be made with several methods, including this method that measures the presence of magnetic properties of different molecules as they move about in a very strong magnetic field. This method does not produce X-rays and it does not use radioactive markers, so it is believed to be very safe for most people.

genes—A permanent set of about 20,000 separate instructions or blueprints for the structures (proteins and other molecules) that build our bodies and catalysts (enzymes) that actually run the individual cells.

medications—Substances, usually prescribed by trained and licensed physicians, which have been studied for curative properties.

mood state—From despair to elation, mood states reflect our attitude toward our lives and people around us.

neurotransmitter—A chemical key that travels across a synapse to reach a receptor molecule, where formation of a signal to the next cell can get started. Some molecules (natural or otherwise) activate receptors, while others can block the site for the true transmitters. Substances of abuse can compete with endogenous (natural) molecules for the same site, causing changes in mood and other behaviors.

neurotransmitter metabolites—Metabolites are inactive enzyme products resulting from a breakdown of the neurotransmitters. The breakdown cannot occur while the transmitter is inside a protective vesicle. Release from the vesicle is necessary for signaling the next cell and leaves the transmitter vulnerable to the actions of enzymes that change it to these inactive forms.

neurotransmitter release—Neurotransmitters are released from vesicle packets inside the cell when the vesicle walls fuse with the cell membrane, creating an exit pore for the neurotransmitter. The free neurotransmitter can migrate to nearby cell membranes, including the cell that it came from, and give a signal to receptors on the cell membranes.

odds ratio (OR)—The relative increase in likelihood of an event. An OR of one means there is no change in the likelihood. When the OR is two, the likelihood is doubled.

panic disorder—Panic disorder, one specific form of anxiety, can be associated with suicidal behavior. Feelings of shortness of breath, hyperventilation, shakiness or dizziness, racing heartbeat or pounding in the chest, and a feeling of impending doom associated with severe, sudden waves of anxiety. Sometimes it is accompanied by agoraphobia, the fear of crowded places. This illness responds quite well to talk therapy or to medications.

personality traits—Characteristics making up an individual's identity; how each of us responds to events, situations, and other people. Traits are firmly established by the age of 18, and are likely to remain constant throughout life unless addressed, usually in talk therapies.

risk factors—Those events or behaviors that are signs of danger and are associated with increased suicidal thinking or attempts. Certain mental disorders, called internal risks, include depression, bipolar disorder, substance abuse, stress, and conduct disorder. External risks include personal illness, illnesses or deaths in the family, childhood abuse, and divorce.

schizophrenia—This is an emotional illness in which very severe distortions of reality, that can include visions or hearing voices, can appear in the absence of sadness or other mood changes. There are many possible causes of hallucinations, so that a long period of observation is required before this diagnosis can be made.

serotonin—A small molecule made of carbon, nitrogen, oxygen, and hydrogen that carries signaling information between cells in almost all living things. It was discovered in the mid-20th century and was originally thought to simply regulate the small muscles in the walls of arteries. It is important in many organ systems, especially the intestines and the brain. It is implicated in the causal pathways of mental illnesses.

synapse—A very narrow gap, about 20 nanometers wide (five one-hundred-thousandths of an inch), between a nerve terminal membrane and a nerve dendrite.

suicide—The act of willfully taking a course of action or inaction that causes one's own death.

talk therapy—A part of the treatment of mental disorders where a trained professional helps his or her clients to understand what they feel, why, and how to set goals for change, as well as to recognize risk behaviors. Therapists work with individuals, couples, families, or groups. Therapists may specialize in one or more method, including cognitive-behavioral therapy (CBT); dialectical behavior therapy (DBT); group therapy; interpersonal therapy (IPT); and psychoanalytically based psychotherapy, among others.

transporter—A protein that is used to move ions or molecules across a cell membrane. In neuron cells, a reuptake transporter is used to vacuum up transmitters (such as serotonin, norepinephrine, and dopamine) for recycling and rerelease into the synapse at another time. It is similar in concept to the transporter on *Star Trek*, with the neurotransmitter molecule being pulled back through a specially dedicated gate in the cell membrane.

tryptophan—An amino acid that is needed to make serotonin.

turnover—Because neurotransmitters are recycled for reuse, the amount of transmitter release is difficult to measure directly. When the transmitter is irreversibly converted to a waste product that is easy to measure, scientists use the phrase "measure the turnover."

Suicide Prevention Hotline

National Hopeline Network
(800) SUI-CIDE or (800) 784-2433

Books

Blauner, Susan Rose. *How I Stayed Alive When My Brain Was Trying to Kill Me: One Person's Guide to Suicide Prevention.* New York: William Morrow, 2002.

Elkind, David. *The Hurried Child: Growing Up Too Fast Too Soon.* 3d ed. New York: Perseus Publishing, 2001.

Portner, Jessica. *One in Thirteen: The Silent Epidemic of Teen Suicide.* Beltsville, Md.: Robins Lane Press, 2001.

Film

"The Truth About Suicide: Real Stories of Depression in College" (27 minutes)
American Foundation for Suicide Prevention
http://www.afsp.org/collegefilm
(888) 333-AFSP

Web Sites

American Academy of Pediatrics

http://www.aap.org/advocacy/childhealthmonth/prevteensuicide.htm

"Some Things You Should Know About Preventing Teen Suicide" is an excellent resource containing a very usable list of warning signs for teen depression and suicidal thoughts.

American Foundation for Suicide Prevention

http://www.afsp.org/index.cfm?page_id=056954D8-0D84-0DD0-4984862095B0D073

Among many initiatives, the Teen Suicide Prevention Campaign is specifically promoted by AFSP. The home site, http://www.afsp.org, is user friendly, leading quickly to helpful information about a variety of specific topics.

American Psychiatric Association

http://www.healthyminds.org/multimedia/teensuicide.pdf

About Teen Suicide, a brochure in the Let's Talk Facts series, is geared toward parents and school professionals. Other informative discussions about treatment are available on the main Web site of the American Psychiatric Association.

Focus Adolescent Services

http://www.focusas.com/Suicide.html

A site that is highly rated and a reliable clearinghouse from an organization specifically oriented toward needs and issues of adolescents.

The Forney Center: Housing for Homeless Lesbian, Gay, Bisexual, and Transgendered (LGBT) Youth

http://www.aliforneycenter.org/

More than an emergency service, the Ali Forney Center offers mental health assessment and care, transitional housing, education, and outreach services to families of LGBT youths ages 16-24.

National Institute of Mental Health and Centers for Disease Control and Prevention

http://www.nimh.nih.gov/suicideprevention/suicidefaq.cfm
http://www.cdc.gov/ncipc/factsheets/suifacts.htm
http://www.cdc.gov/mmwr/preview/mmwrhtml/mm5526a1.htm

All are outstanding, highly readable, and informative sites sponsored by government health agencies. The first site is in a question-and-answer format that should be helpful for individuals with suicidal thoughts as well as parents and peers. The second site has a lengthy discussion of suicide, including facts about groups at risk for suicide or suicide attempts, risk factors, and prevention strategies, among other topics. The third site describes data from the federal Centers for Disease Control and Prevention.

Psych Central

http://psychcentral.com/

A highly reliable resource for finding Web sites on many mental disorders.

Columbia University TeenScreen Program

http://www.teenscreen.org/

A screening program for youths to evaluate their mental health and suicide risk, as well as to educate them and adults on relevant topics. The 10-minute questionnaire, HealthScreen, is online yet school or parental supervision is strongly recommended.

INDEX

CBT. *See* cognitive-behavioral therapy

Centers for Disease Control (CDC), 74

chemical imbalance, 17–21, 45–49, 72–73.
    See also brain chemistry

children, 74, 86

choking, 41–42

chronic illness, 6–7, 51, 54–60

cigarettes, 11

Cipriani, Andrea, 84

cognitive-behavioral therapy (CBT),
    33, 87

cognitive rigidity, 39

Columbia Health Screen, 68

combined treatment (talk therapy and
    medication), 13–15, 76, 78, 85–86, 88

coming out, 57

communication
    Carla's issues, 49–52
    and depression treatment, 44, 45
    importance of, 90
    and impulsive behavior, 23–24
    lack of, as obstacle, 26–27
    as therapy goal, 49–53

confused thoughts, 15

control, in depression study, 81–82, 97

corticosteroids, 86

Costello, Jane, 9

Crosby, A. E., 66

David (case study), 6–7, 15, 54–59

DBT (dialectical behavior therapy), 87

Delgado, Pedro, 45

delusions, 64

depression, 5, 41–45
    in adolescents, 33
    and anxiety, 30
    atypical, 80–82
    and brain chemistry/structure, 5, 18–22,
        45–49, 79–80
    and brain damage, 50–51
    and Carla's suicide attempt, 4, 6
    defined, 97

effects on behavior, 80

in the elderly, 69

medication for. *See* antidepressants

research on subtypes of, 79–83

as risk factor, 9, 61, 64, 65

as side effect of various medications, 77

and stroke, 72

and suicide rates, 74–75

and tendency not to seek treatment,
    73–74

and UBOs, 50

desipramine, 87

diabetes, 54–58

dialectical behavior therapy (DBT), 87

diazepam, 36

diet, serotonin production and, 45–48

disabilities, *59*

disruptive disorder, 9, 61–62

divorce, 23–24

DNA (deoxyribonucleic acid), 18

dopamine-blocking drugs, 36

Doucette, Steve, 85

drinking. *See* alcohol

drug abuse. *See* substance abuse

drug trials, 75–76

dual diagnosis, 9, 42

dysthymia, 5

elderly, 26, 69

electroconvulsive therapy (ECT), 80, 98

emergency room, 69

environment, 40

external risk factors, 8, 11

family, 10, 11, 16

females, 66, 68, 69

Fergusson, Dean, 85

firearms. *See* guns

Foley, Debra, 9

food, and serotonin production,
    45–48

Food and Drug Administration, 75

multiple risk factors, 65
multiple sclerosis (MS), 50, 51, 83, 87

Native Americans, 66, 67
nervous breakdown, 8
neurotransmitter, 18, 40, 72–73, 81, 98
norepinephrine reuptake inhibitors
    (NRIs), 36
norepinephrine serotonin reuptake
    inhibitors (NSRIs), 36
nutrition, and serotonin production,
    45–48

overdose, 2, 28, 34, 84

pancreatic cancer, 51
panic, 3, 28, 31–33, *32*, 99
Parkinson's disease, 50–51
Paxil, 37
permissive effects, 85
pessimism, 41–45
PET scan, of brain, *5*
pharmaceutical industry, research by,
    75–77
physical abuse, 16
plans, for suicide, 34–35
predictors, 46–47
preteen children, 86
protective factors, 47
Prozac, *37*
psychiatric illnesses, 9
psychodynamic psychotherapy, 87

rates, of suicide, 1, 8, 26, 63, 74–75
reasons, for suicide attempts, 1–16
recurrence
    of depression, 4, 5
    of suicidal thoughts, 65
resperine, 77
risk factors, 61–73
    in Abe's suicide attempt, 2
    for adolescents, 65, 69–70

for adults, 66
brain injury, 70–72, 71
defined, 99
for elderly, 69
family history, 16
for females, 66
historical, 16
for males, 66
medications as source of, 43–45, 76–77,
    84–86
predictors, 46–47
psychiatric illnesses, 9
and treatment, 73–77
for youth, 66–68
romantic relationships, 2, 23–24
Rothblum, Esther, 56

Saperia, J., 84
schizophrenia, 8, 99
second generation antidepressants, 78
second messengers, 81
selective serotonin reuptake inhibitors
    (SSRIs), *37*
self-esteem, low, 73–74
serotonin, *19*
    defined, 99
    and depression, 40
    and diet, 45–48
    genes related to, 21, 22
    and lithium, 37
    as neurotransmitter substance, 18, 20
    in suicide victims, 40
serotonin reuptake inhibitors (SRIs), 36,
    78, 84–85
sexual abuse, 16, 64
sexual orientation, 6–7, 54, 56–57
side effects, 77, 78, 88
SLC6A4 gene, 20
sleep patterns, 23, 80
smoking, 11
SRIs. *See* serotonin reuptake
    inhibitors